The
Connell Guide
to
T. S. Eliot's

The Waste Land

by
Seamus Perry

Contents

Introduction

The Waste Land, first published in 1922, is not far from a century old, and it has still not been surpassed as the most famous and, moreover, the most exemplary of all modern poems. In many ways, it continues to define what we mean by modern whenever we begin to speak about modern verse. Part of that modernity lies in the way it is sometimes referred to as a difficult poem; but, at the same time, as Ted Hughes once observed, without denying its genuine kinds of difficulty, it is also genuinely popular, and not just among the cogniscenti or the degree-bearing. "I remember when I taught fourteen-year-old boys in a secondary modern school," Hughes once said, "of all the poetry I introduced them to, their favourite was *The Waste Land.*"

My own experience as a tutor confirms that students – once they allow themselves to become immersed in its rhythms and patterns, and as they begin to worry less about obscurity and start attuning themselves instead to the interplay of its voices – take to the poem in a way they do to few others. Not for nothing was it included, in its entirety, in Helen Gardner's *New Oxford Book of English Verse* (1972), a decision replicated in *The Oxford Book of Twentieth Century English Verse* (1973), edited by Philip Larkin, a poet not known otherwise for his hospitality to modernism. For the poem has indeed achieved what Eliot had conceived as an ideal: it is a committed work of the imagination that manages to speak to the broadest constituency of readers, as an Elizabethan play engaged the whole theatre.

Wordsworth hoped for a work of "Joy in widest commonalty spread"; and commonalty might seem in as short supply as joy in *The Waste Land*; but in truth it shares the predicament it imagines with all the generosity, self-awareness, and inclusive tact of Wordsworth at his most characteristic. The poem's appeal is intellectual, certainly, but also visceral, as much about rhythms as it is about references; it is by turns wittily cerebral, ugly, tender, disabused, damaged, resilient, poignant. It is a place where you come across lines with all the barren immediacy of

> *Here is no water but only rock*
> *Rock and no water and the sandy road*

and the brilliantly psychologised horror poetry of

> *her hair*
> *Spread out in fiery points*
> *Glowed into words, then would be savagely still*

but find, also, an unexpected lyrical loveliness that
uplifts a wholly contemporary kind of perception –
"Trams and dusty trees" – a powerfully
unproclaimed sympathy:

> *After the event*
> *He wept. He promised 'a new start.'*
> *I made no comment. What should I resent?*

It fulfils in miniature the demands that Eliot
made of the great poet at large: "abundance, variety,
and complete competence" – the first of those
criteria of greatness all the more surprising, and
moving, to find accomplished in a poem that has its
starting place in so barren a human territory.

The poetry is modern in a wholly self-conscious
way, just as James Joyce's *Ulysses* bears the marks
of its own ingenious self-invention on every page;
and, like Joyce's masterpiece, the modernity of
Eliot's poem stems in large part from a strikingly
powerful awareness of what's past. My aim in this
short book has been primarily to point out some of
the fruits of that acute historical awareness –
besides, I hope, sharing some of my own admiration
of, and pleasure in, the extraordinary voicings and
counter-voicings of this perpetually great work.

A summary of the plot

The Waste Land is a modernist poem and not a piece of narrative so it does not have a *plot* exactly; but, full of thoughts of Shakespeare as it is, its division into five movements might dimly remind us of the five progressive acts of a play; and it certainly has a trajectory of a kind. The poem has not always appeared that way: some reviewers thought it lacked any shape at all. Conrad Aiken, an astute familiar of Eliot's from Harvard, announced in his review of the first edition that "we must with reservations, and with no invidiousness, conclude that the poem is not, in any formal sense, coherent". F.R. Leavis, an early champion, asserted: "It exhibits no progression."

After several decades of dedicated critical and scholarly labour and ingenuity, there are probably few admirers of Eliot now who would say so quite so flatly: the poem has come across in most critical accounts for the last 50 or more years as a fully coherent piece of art, even if the coherence in question is sometimes a matter of an intently deconstructive self-consciousness. Indeed it is perhaps possible for criticism to make the poem feel a little *too* thoroughly organised, thus missing out on something of that sense of rebarbativeness and dissonance to which its early readers often responded, and which probably still forms an important part of the feelings of most people they encounter it for the first time.

"The progress in *The Waste Land*, for there is progress," Helen Gardner said in one of the most helpful early books on Eliot, "is not the progress of narrative, movement along a line, the progress of an Odysseus towards his home or of Bunyan's pilgrim from the City of Destruction to the Celestial City." It is, she says, rather, "a deeper and deeper exploration of an original scene or theme", which usefully conveys both a sense of progressing somewhere purposefully and a sense of getting nowhere fast at the same time.

So how should we try to understand its organisation? Aiken himself went on to suggest in his review that "Mr Eliot is perhaps attempting a kind of program music in words" – as though he were emulating a tone poem by Richard Strauss, such as *Don Quixote* or *Till Eulenspiegel*, in which the music seeks, without using words, to describe episodes in the title character's story and to evoke the fluctuations of his adventuresome emotions.

The Waste Land has many characters, not just one; but, as Eliot's own note to line 218 observes, in a way all the characters are parts of a single consciousness or, as Eliot says, a little mysteriously, "personage"; and while no narrative exactly, you can see the poem as a symbolic depiction of the vicissitudes of that consciousness. The musical analogy has appealed to many critics: "the organisation which it achieves as a work of art...

may be called musical", said Leavis. "If it were desired to label in three words the most characteristic feature of Mr Eliot's technique," said I.A. Richards, "this might be done by calling his poetry a 'music of ideas'." (Both were picking up a theme from Eliot himself, who spoke in several places about the parallel between music and poetry.)

Allowing for the obvious difficulties, here is an attempt to summarise the plot of the poem, to many points of which I shall be returning later in this book.

I. The Burial of the Dead

The poem opens with a voice, unidentified, apparently speaking on behalf of an 'us', also unidentified, characterising the coming of spring in a starkly counter-intuitive way, as the unwanted re-imposition of a vitality happily lost through the dormancy of the preceding winter. This voice then merges, unannounced, into a recollection of episodes that occurred, at some unspecified time, in Munich and on vacation in the mountains: the poem only lets us know that a speaker is called 'Marie', a member of a grand family. The verse then goes through another transition, both in register and location: now the voice emerges from a dry and stony desert, invoking a biblical resonance in its address to "Son of Man" (which comes from Ezekiel) to whom a prophetic voice promises to show "fear in a handful of dust".

The next episode, the recollection of a desperately tongue-tied encounter between the speaker and a young woman, comes framed by two bits of German, both taken from Wagner's great love opera *Tristan and Isolde*. And then another abrupt change: we hear a dubious clairvoyante, Madame Sosostris, casting someone a fortune with a pack of tarot cards; and then another: a different 'I' again remembers crossing London Bridge, bumping into an old acquaintance, and enquiring in what seems a deranged way about a bit of bizarre gardening: "That corpse you planted last year in your garden, / Has it begun to sprout?"

II. A Game of Chess

Eliot offers a diptych of female portraits. The first, which opens with an allusion to Shakespeare's Cleopatra, describes a woman in an immensely elaborate and thickly odorous drawing room; she is described in a confusingly ornate and sophisticated syntax; a painting on the wall depicts an ancient story of sexual violence. She conducts a fraught, one-sided non-conversation with a man, presumably her husband, whose thoughts remain darkly unarticulated. Then, jumping to the other side of London, a second study portrays a woman talking in a pub as closing time approaches: she has a tangled and inconsequential story to tell about a friend, Lil, and the homecoming of Lil's husband, Albert, after his time in the army during the Great War. The section ends with the drinkers ejected from the pub, bidding each other goodnight.

III. The Fire Sermon

A view of the desolate Thames, described in an anonymous voice haunted by poetry of the English Renaissance (Edmund Spenser, Andrew Marvell, Shakespeare). The heterogeneity of the succeeding verse is disorientating: a scrap of an obscene ballad about a brothel-keeper; a lovely line from the French poet Paul Verlaine; some uprooted fragments of Elizabethan English; a *non sequitur* of a story about an ambiguous encounter with a merchant from Smyrna. And then we arrive at what Eliot's note describes as "the substance of the poem", narrated by a version of Tiresias, an aged blind prophet from Greek myth: he watches the seduction of a typist by an opportunistic "house agent's clerk", and gently intuits her thoughts after the clerk has gone.

Another 'I' enters the poem, recalling the sound of music from another London pub, and the glory of the interior of a London church; and then we return to an evocation of the Thames, both the contemporary waterway of "Oil and tar" and the glittering river of the reign of Elizabeth I. Wagner now returns to the poem, this time with a quotation from his opera cycle *The Ring*, which opens with the singing of the three beautiful Rhinemaidens. Except Eliot offers us not Rhinemaidens but Thames maidens, whose unhappy experiences in love are charted down the length of the urban river, from Richmond and Kew in Surrey down to its estuary, where the river empties out into the sea, at Margate in Kent. Descending now into the poem's greatest moment of studied incoherence, some scraps of St Augustine juxtapose abruptly with a repeated fragment of the Buddha's Fire Sermon; and at this point of linguistic near-collapse, the section closes in fire.

IV. Death by Water

A short section describes the physical dissolution of one Phlebas, a sailor from Phoenicia, whose corpse has fallen apart after a fortnight in the ocean. A moralising voice warns the reader to remember his example.

V. What the Thunder said

The opening lines evoke an arid desert-scape with a reiterative, sparse power. We tune in, briefly, to the voice of a traveller, whose journey is mysteriously haunted by an elusive third figure whose presence is felt but who can never be observed. With a startling change of perspective, a bleak panorama opens up of crowds swarming over the "endless plains" of a ruined Europe; in a no less startling change, some vampiric figure briefly enters the poem; and in a further transition, the poem focuses in on an abandoned chapel, its door swinging in the dry wind.

At this point, in a poem that has been full of aridity, rain seems about to arrive, and the thunder that heralds its appearance speaks in Sanskrit. The noise of the thunder is interpreted as the first syllable of a word of moral instruction in three ways: as "Datta", meaning 'give'; as "Dayadhvam", meaning 'sympathise'; and as "Damyata", meaning 'control' (according to Eliot's note). After each of these routes to spiritual transformation is announced, the poem hesitantly responds to their challenge, one by one: in the giving that would be constituted by "The awful daring of a moment's surrender"; in the sympathy that would overcome the isolation of the individual, each locked in the prison of himself; and in the control that would have arisen in a loving response that (as the grammar conveys) never occurred.

The poem then invokes its presiding landscape, "the arid plain", for the last time, before an extraordinary crescendo of apparently heterogeneous fragments taken from nursery rhymes, Latin poetry, Dante, Thomas Kyd and others; and the poem closes with a final invocation from the Sanskrit: "Shantih shantih shantih", which, as Eliot's note tells us, is the formal close to an Upanishad, meaning ""The Peace which passeth understanding" is our equivalent to this word" – or, as the first edition of the poem had it, "'The Peace which passeth understanding' is a feeble translation of the content of this word". (Eliot was confirmed in the Church of England in 1927.) The poem has certainly glimpsed the grounds for such peace in its closing passages, and there is some feel to the last pages of a journey being completed; but *The Waste Land* can hardly be said to have won its way through to consolation in any straightforward way, and Eliot's programme music does not end with an untroubled major chord.

What is *The Waste Land* about?

Eliot was typically self-deprecatory about any momentous claims made for his poetry. "I am used to having cosmic significances, which I never suspected, extracted from my work (such as it is) by enthusiastic persons at a distance," he once half-mock-lamented. *The Waste Land* has had more than its share of cosmic significances extracted, often about the sick soul of Western man. "Various critics have done me the honour to interpret the poem in terms of criticism of the contemporary world," he is reported to have said later in life, adding: "To me it was only the relief of a personal and wholly insignificant grouse against life; it is just a piece of rhythmical grumbling."

ELIOT IN THE BANK

After some time as a school teacher – where he had John Betjeman among his pupils, something remembered in Betjeman's verse autobiography *Summoned by Bells* – Eliot took a job in Lloyds Bank in March 1917. He enjoyed the post: "It is a great satisfaction to me to have regular work," he told his mother; and he was evidently good at it. In 1918, he attempted to volunteer for both the United States army and navy, without success, and his employers were pleased to see him back and

One should never be too ready to take Eliot's self-deprecation (or, indeed, anyone's) at face value; but he was certainly right that people were ready to interpret the poem from the beginning as the statement of the dismay of an epoch. "The agony and bitter splendor of modern life are in this poem," as the editor Harriet Monroe put it, saying what lots of people felt – F.R. Leavis, for example, who found a keen expression of "our present plight ... the final uprooting of the immemorial ways of life, of life rooted in the soil... the troubles of the present age" (*New Bearings in English Poetry*, 1932) or I.A. Richards, who described the poem as "a clearer, fuller realisation of... the plight of a whole generation, than they find elsewhere".

Eliot would come to regard this sort of reaction among his appreciative early readers as

set him on "new and more intricate work"; by the beginning of 1920 his salary had been raised to £500, a mark of how highly he was regarded. "I am supposed to be a profound economist," he told his mother, comically; but he was accomplished enough to be entrusted with sorting out some of the many complications of Germany's war debts, "and trying to elucidate knotty points in that appalling document the Peace Treaty". The sense of the fragmentation of modern Europe which infests the poem was drawn from more than an acquaintance with the newspapers.

Aldous Huxley visited him and found "the most bank-clerky of all bank clerks. He was not on the ground floor nor even on the floor under that, but in a sub-sub-basement sitting at a desk which was in a row of desks with other bank clerks." Ezra "nonsense": "I may have expressed for them their own illusion of being disillusioned, but that did not form part of my intention." Nevertheless, despite his later remarks, such an epochal impression was not simply the work of cranky or wilful misreading for Eliot evidently worked into his poem material drawn from wide realms of modern history and politics: the poem is acutely conscious, for example, that its stage is contemporary Europe, in the aftermath of the Great War and amid the confusions of a troubled peace. In his notes to the poem, Eliot adduces Herman Hesse's recent book *In Sight of Chaos* (1920), a book which charismatically portrays a Europe going down the tubes fast; and a sense of the important contemporaneity of the poem is bolstered by Eliot's admiration for Joyce's newly published

Pound was no less dismayed by such employment: "it is a crime against literature to let him waste eight hours vitality per diem in that bank"; and he attempted, unsuccessfully, to raise funds from wealthy admirers to buy Eliot out, somewhat to Eliot's consternation.

When his health finally broke in the autumn of 1921 the bank gave Eliot paid leave to recuperate, "very generously", as he remarked; and when he finally returned to London in January 1922 after his visit to Paris, with the manuscript of his poem now improved by Pound, he went back to work at the bank, where he would stay until, in 1925, he joined the new firm of Faber and Gwyer (later Faber and Faber) as a publisher.

He would become one of the most influential publishers of poetry in the novel *Ulysses* (1922) and its depiction of "the immense panorama of futility and anarchy which is contemporary history" – not very true to the feel of Joyce's Dublin, in fact, but a good description of the world of Eliot's poem.

Among the other errors in interpretation that his poetry had encountered, Eliot later said, were "having my personal biography reconstructed from passages which I got out of books, or which I invented out of nothing because they sounded well; and to having my biography invariably ignored in what I *did* write from personal experience". Mary Hutchinson, who knew Eliot, certainly took the main reference of *The Waste Land* to be personal: "Tom's autobiography", she wrote after hearing the poem, "a melancholy one". It is a poem centrally preoccupied by the failure of

20th century; but it was banking's loss. While visiting him at Lloyds once day, I.A Richards was quizzed by one of the senior staff about the merits of Eliot's work. Richards assured him that Eliot was indeed, in Richards's view, a good poet. The banker, who comes out of the story very well I think, expressed relief and offered an institution's tribute: "I believe that anything a man does, whatever his hobby may be, it's all the better if he is really keen on it and does it well. I think it helps him with his work. If you see our young friend, you might tell him that we think he's doing quite well at the Bank. In fact, if he goes on as he has been doing, I don't see why – in time, of course, in time – he mightn't even become a Branch Manager." "Most gratifying," remarked Eliot, upon hearing the report ■

human relationships; and it was no secret to any of his circle at the time that Eliot's marriage to Vivien Haigh-Wood was failing. (Towards the end of his life he would write in a private paper: "To her the marriage brought no happiness... to me, it brought the state of mind out of which came *The Waste Land*.")

But to interpret the poem merely as an expression of Eliot's local melancholy would be seriously to undersell the amplitude of the poem's ambition. Likewise, it is a poem that seems to report back from a fraught religious life, or a life troubled by the ghostly presence of a richer sort of life that cannot be led; and Eliot was, according to a remark of his that Stephen Spender later overheard, seriously considering becoming a Buddhist at the time he was working on the poem. But it would be as unsatisfactory to interpret the poem as incipiently Buddhist as it would be to see it as leaning towards the Christian dawn that finally broke when Eliot joined the Church. In fact, the poem works assiduously to evade religious affiliations: its instincts are, as we shall see, purposefully ecumenical, combining Western and Eastern traditions.

Fortunately we do not need to choose between reading the poem either as the articulation of the consciousness of an age or as the expression of a wholly personal crisis. When Eliot said a few years afterwards that the "great poet, in writing himself,

Eliot as a young man sailing (1907)

writes his time", it is tempting to think he did so
with a sense of what he had pulled off in the great
poem, the genius of which had been to find in
the depths of individual unhappiness a way of
articulating a sense of anxiety and rootlessness
that did feel generational – rather as Tennyson's
In Memoriam had done 75 years earlier for the

Victorians, and, as Eliot said, John Donne had done for the intellectuals of the Elizabethan age. "Donne is difficult to analyse," he wrote in the same year as *The Waste Land*: "what appears at one time a curious personal point of view may at another time appear rather the precise concentration of a kind of feeling diffused in the air about him" ('Andrew Marvell'). Eliot's poem thrives on a similar brand of enabling difficulty. Eliot wrote to his father at Christmas 1917 from a London preoccupied by the war in Europe: "everyone's individual lives are so swallowed up in the one great tragedy, that one almost ceases to have personal experiences or emotions, and such as one has seem so unimportant!" The different tragedy of life after the War was to prove no less all-encompassing.

THE ROLE OF EZRA POUND

The Waste Land drew in small part on material that Eliot had written long before, but the main composition of the poem began in late January or early February 1921, with Parts I and II typed up in May. The beginning of Part III was written during the summer; but by the end of August Eliot's health was failing. He consulted a specialist at the end of September and was told to have three months of complete rest, so he took leave of absence from Lloyds Bank, and from the middle of October he stayed for almost

What does the epigraph do?

Eliot's work comes with an epigraph, taken from a Latin prose work entitled the *Satyricon* by Petronius. It is a quotation from a long section in which many stories are told by guests at a boozy dinner party hosted by a vulgarian named Trimalchio, who braggingly tells the anecdote from which the epigraph is taken. It describes an encounter with the Cumean Sibyl, a famous prophet who was granted eternal life but, having forgotten to request perennial youth, endlessly suffered the painful degradations of old age. The speaker boasts: "Once I saw with my very own eyes the Cumean Sybil hanging in a jar." She is asked, in Greek: "Sibyl, what do you want?" And she replies:

a month in the seaside resort of Margate (mentioned in the poem at l.300), at first in company with his wife, but then solitarily, during which time he wrote several sections destined for Part III.

After a brief stay in London, he travelled via Paris to Lausanne, where he was to stay for six weeks under the care of a psychiatrist whom had been especially recommended to him. It was here that he finished the original draft of the poem.

He arrived in Paris on January 1922 and handed the manuscript over to Ezra Pound. Pound (1885-1972) was also an American who had left for Europe, a poet with a select reputation, a critic of erratic brilliance, and a literary impresario of real genius. It was Pound who had spotted 'Prufrock' and got it published, admiring Eliot as a fellow modern: "He has actually trained himself

"I want to die."

Many works have epigraphs, of course; it is a gesture to a more normal sort of literature; and this one, like any good epigraph, is an oblique clue about what to expect next. It comes from an ancient literary work which, though a thing of high larks, is nevertheless an anticipation of the poem to follow in that it is made up of an array of different voices – different languages, even, as here – woven together, each saying their own thing and contributing to a single work at the same time. The epigraph powerfully voices the longing for oblivion that haunts many of Eliot's lines too, foreshadowing especially the figure of Tiresias who will appear in Part III, and it does so specifically in the form of female suffering, which will prove so central an element in the poem. So it seems to fit very well.

AND modernized himself ON HIS OWN," he wrote admiringly.

Now Pound had some work to do: "Eliot came back from his Lausanne specialist looking OK; and with a damn good poem (19 pages) in his suitcase." His admiration grew upon acquaintance: "About enough, Eliot's poem, to make the rest of us shut up shop." Eliot trusted Pound's judgment, and accepted most (not all) of his numerous suggested changes to the text.

There were many small amendments in phrasing. Pound disapproved of the word "perhaps": "Perhaps be damned," he wrote next to one of Eliot's more cautious formulations; and, later on, next to the draft line (which became l.251) "Across her mind one half-formed

But, as it happens, we know from the surviving manuscripts that Petronius was not Eliot's first choice for the epigraph: he had originally chosen a passage from Joseph Conrad's novel *Heart of Darkness* (1899). This novel takes the form of a long story, narrated by a seaman called Marlow while he sits on a boat on the Thames one darkening evening, describing an expedition to the Congo in which he had participated years earlier. The climax of his narration is the discovery of the monstrous Kurtz, an ivory trader who has gone savagely mad after a protracted period in the depths of the jungle. Kurtz's death is reported by Marlow:

> Did he live his life again in every detail of desire, temptation, and surrender during that supreme moment of complete knowledge? He cried in a

thought may pass", Pound scribbled: "make up yr. mind you Tiresias if you know [,] know damn well or else you don't". He also cut some of the disgusted excesses; in the original, the house-agent's clerk pauses on his way home "to urinate, and spit". Pound ran a line through the couplet, remarking: "proba[b]ly over the mark".

There were also some large excisions. The narrative opening to the poem, describing a boozy brothel crawl in Boston, was cut; as was the Popean satirical portrait of 'Fresca' that opened Part III; the long account of a sea voyage ending in shipwreck that constituted most of Part IV also went.

The poem as re-shaped by Pound is pretty much the

whisper at some image, at some vision – he cried
out twice, a cry that was not more than a breath –
"The horror! the horror!"

Eliot admired the passage greatly and thought
it "much the most appropriate I can find, and
somewhat elucidative" as an epigraph. He was
put off by his friend and mentor Ezra Pound,
who momentarily wondered whether Conrad was
sufficiently "weighty" for the job; and while most
of Pound's editorial interventions were brilliant,
I wonder if Eliot's first instinct was not right
here. (Valerie Eliot later remembered that Eliot
regretted changing his mind.) Like the overture to
an opera, the Conrad passage would have offered
a first glimpse of some of the poem's recurrent
elements: 'desire', 'temptation', and 'surrender', for

poem as we have it, with the
exception of the new opening
to Part III, which Eliot wrote
while in Paris to replace
Fresca. ("Do something
different," was Pound's firm
advice.) All in all, Pound's
attentions amount to what is
"widely recognized as one of
the greatest acts of editorial
intervention on record", in
Lawrence Rainey's
persuasive verdict. Eliot
honoured Pound with the
dedication to the poem: "*il
miglior fabbro*" – "the better
craftsman" – Dante's tribute
to the Provençal poet Arnaut
Daniel, who makes a fleeting
purgatorial appearance at
l.427 of the poem.

The fate of the manuscript
is a curious story. Eliot
presented it to his patron, the
wealthy New York lawyer
John Quinn, as a mark of his
appreciation for aiding the
publication of the poem in
America. After Quinn died in
July 1924 his estate passed

a start; but also a number of the key words which, threaded through the poem, constitute one of its main organising principles – 'moment', 'whisper', 'image'; and the reference in Part I to "the heart of light" would have had a likely context confirmed. Not least, the whole idea of an account of primeval darkness told against the parallel darkness of contemporary London has an important precedent in Conrad. But anyway, the passage went, one of many changes that Pound made to the drafts of the poem that he received in the early days of 1922.

How are we to read the epigraph?

In a way, the presence of an epigraph matters more to *The Waste Land* than it does to most works, because it works as a quick tutorial in the way that

down his family; but the manuscript of Eliot's poem cannot have been regarded as much of a treasure since it seems to have been left in storage for years, to be re-discovered only in the 1950s. It was subsequently sold to the New York Public Library. Neither Eliot nor Pound were told of the sale, and indeed no one beyond the Library seems to have known about it either until the news was belatedly broken in 1968. The re-appearance made something of a splash, finally solving what Pound satirically referred to as "The mystery of the missing manuscript" – "pure Henry James", he thought. A handsome edition of the manuscripts, with photographs of the originals and transcriptions of their complicated texts, was produced by Valerie, Eliot's second wife and widow, in 1971 ∎

the poem is going to work. *The Waste Land* builds up meaning by juxtaposing apparently incongruous and incompatible elements, and inviting or challenging or daring the reader to search out the links that might make sense of it. This may appear strikingly audacious as a way of proceeding, and it is certainly at the furthest remove from writing such as discursive prose or poetry that sets out to *say* something that we might carry away and call to mind later in our own paraphrase. Some have found the Eliot method deeply irritating just because of this marked distance from normal communication. The gifted and witty critic Graham Hough, for instance, once denounced the technique, rising to this fine crescendo:

> To attempt to explain to an intelligent person who knows nothing about twentieth-century poetry how *The Waste Land* works is to be overcome with embarrassment at having to justify principles so affected, so perverse, so deliberately removed from the ordinary modes of rational communication.

Eliot sometimes conveyed the impression that poetry did indeed work in a different way to the ordinary modes of language. He spoke in one

Portrait of Ezra Pound by Wyndham Lewis, 1920

place, for instance, of a "logic of the imagination" that he contrasted with "the logic of concepts"; and anecdotes survive of his stylish inscrutability when asked to spell things out. Asked the meaning of the line "Lady, three white leopards sat under a juniper tree" (from 'Ash-Wednesday'), he is reported to have looked at his questioner and replied: "I meant 'Lady, three white leopards sat under a juniper tree'." Taking such an approach seriously would mean giving up criticism, or even talking about books, altogether: which might be a price thought worth paying, of course; but there are other reasons to resist the suggestion that Eliot's language is peculiarly impenetrable in the ways it creates meaning.

For while obviously innovative, in another way Eliot is merely – 'merely', except no one else thought to do it – applying the familiar logic of the epigraph to the making of poetry at large. Consider, for example, the epigraph that stands at the head of Eliot's early masterpiece 'The Love Song of J. Alfred Prufrock'. Most readers' eyes skip over the Italian, I suppose, and alight with a proper pleasure on the wonder of its opening lines:

> Let us go then, you and I,
> When the evening is spread out against the sky
> Like a patient etherised upon a table

But if you persevere and find out what the Italian

means you discover it is a voice speaking from the depths of Hell – from Dante's *Inferno* – a man who is telling his interlocutor that, were he to believe that anyone had ever returned to earthly life from his terrible eternal home then he would no longer address him; but since, of course, no one has *ever* got back again to the world, he will speak on without fear. (He is not to know that Dante is the only human being in history to have visited Hell and come back to tell the tale.) Only after this terrible speech do we come to: "Let us go then, you and I..." J. Alfred Prufrock and Dante seem as far apart as can be, to be sure, in philosophy as in literary manner; but some subterranean sense of their resemblance animates Eliot's decision to place these texts the one next to the other. What is it? Prufrock inhabits a universe denied the absoluteness of divine judgment that shapes the architecture of Dante's *Commedia*; but, evidently, that does not stop Prufrock inhabiting a hell of his own, one that he believes to be as inescapable as the more familiar damnation suffered by the speaker of the epigraph.

In both its portrayal of broken human relationships and its testing spirituality, *The Waste Land* is, like *The Divine Comedy*, a poem about love, though it approaches that theme by bearing powerful witness to love's evanishment, elusiveness, fragility, and the corrosive power of its distortions. It is, repeatedly, a poem about the failure of men and women to get through to one another, perhaps even to begin to try; and much of the sex-horror in the poem stems from the kinds of false intimacy that desire can forge in the place of genuine connection. Eliot would have shared with E.M. Forster a conviction of the importance of the injunction which stood as epigraph to Forster's novel of 1907, *Howards End*: "Only connect" (to which he may be alluding in l.301). Forster summarises the world-view of one of the characters in his novel approvingly: "Live in fragments no longer. Only connect, and the beast and the monk, robbed of the isolation that is life to either, will die." The spirit of the works is very different, but *The Waste Land* is like *Howards End* in the way it discovers a powerful creative intelligence in the tenderness (also the ferocity) with which it regards the failure of human lives to join up one with another.

Why is *The Waste Land* difficult?

If *The Waste Land* is especially preoccupied by the difficulty of finding connections between one person and another, then the difficulty of its own poetic mode – which invites, and incites, and challenges readers to try and find meaning, by seeing how these strange assemblages of incongruous material might be connected – may seem a less peculiar choice, even an inevitable one. Which is to say: the technique is thoroughly continuous with its moral interest, at once an articulation of, and a contribution to, its meaning. ("We cannot say at what point 'technique' begins or where it ends," said Eliot once.) Virginia Woolf heard Eliot read his poem aloud in June 1922, and straightaway grasped the central truth of the poem with all her usual critical intuition: "It has great beauty & force of phrase: symmetry; & tensity," she wrote in her diary. "What connects it together, I'm not sure." It is far too tough-minded a poem to let us ever be persuaded that we are sure; but it is too humane a poem to withhold from us the possibility that connection might yet be imaginable.

The biographer Lyndall Gordon (in *Eliot's Early Years*) relates the story of Eliot telling a lecture theatre of students that his poetry was "simple and straightforward", and then looking pained when they laughed. Perhaps his audience had been reading one of his essays, written about the time of *The Waste Land*, about the 17th century metaphysical poets, in which Eliot had argued

that it appears likely that poets in our civilization, as it exists at present, must be *difficult*. Our civilization comprehends great variety and complexity, and this variety and complexity, playing upon a refined sensibility, must produce various and complex results. The poet must become more and more comprehensive, more allusive, more indirect, in order to force, to dislocate if necessary, language into his meaning.

F.O. Matthiessen, whose book *The Achievement of T.S. Eliot* (1935) remains one of the most interesting, was ready to agree that "the multiplicity of the modern world" was one of its most telling characteristics: it was a time of "too much", when the human subject encountered "everything at once" and not in the more orderly measure in which experience allegedly arrived in former days.

No doubt it is a kind of modern vanity to assume things are so much more trying now than they used to be; and in fact Eliot's poem is as drawn to establishing continuities between historical and contemporary experience as it is to minding the gap between them; but the perceived sheer complicatedness of modern life – what Eliot's precursor Matthew Arnold called its "hopeless tangle" – is evidently something to which the poem seeks to stay true. One reason that we have come to like the poetry of Donne, Eliot once wrote, was that he seemed to speak to "the apparent irrelevance and unrelatedness of things" which characterises our own minds.

I offer here an anecdote about my late friend, the distinguished Wordsworth scholar Robert Woof, who as a young man studied for a time under Marshall McLuhan, then a famous philosopher of the complexity that he thought uniquely the property of the modern world of print culture. When Robert ventured one morning his hesitations about Eliot's poem, McLuhan called for a copy of the *Toronto Star*, spreading the front page out on the desk: "See, Mr Woof, an article about the economy, a photograph of the Queen, a weather forecast, something afoot in ice hockey, an advertisement for hair tonic, a review of the opera: all these happening at once"; and then a meaningful look – the point being, I suppose, that Eliot's poem had finally captured something of the definitive character of modernity, as captured in the buzzing, juxtapositional, contingent disorder of a newspaper page. It is nice to remember that Eliot's unlikely working title for his poem was 'He Do the Police in Different Voices', a quotation from Dickens's novel *Our Mutual Friend*, in which a character talks fondly about her adopted child's capacity to read out the poly-vocal text of the newspaper so well:

"You mightn't think it, but Sloppy is a beautiful reader of a newspaper," she says. "He do the Police in different voices."

Do we need to spot the references?

The poem is partly difficult, then, in that it is fractured into competing voices that don't identify themselves nor the relationship between them. But there are, as Eliot himself discussed in some detail, all sorts of ways in which poetry can be difficult; and what readers often mean, when faced with *The Waste Land*, is the difficulty they have in getting the references Eliot is making. It is obvious even on first acquaintance that the verse is highly allusive, repeatedly calling other texts and voices into play (that is what 'allusion' means) but without always giving explicit notification of what those texts and voices are, nor what Eliot means to do with them. In the course of its few pages we come across references to the Bible, to the words of the Buddha, and to the Upanishads; to the anthropological writers Frazer and Weston and the philosopher Bradley; to Sappho, Virgil, Ovid, St Augustine, Dante, Chaucer, Malory, Spenser, Kyd, Shakespeare, Webster, Middleton, Milton, Marvell, Dryden, Goldsmith, Tennyson, Baudelaire, Verlaine, Conrad; and several others, either certainly or probably, have their part to play in *The Waste Land*. Does it matter if we do not spot these many allusions?

"It is tactful, when making an obscure reference," said William Empson, who was mindful of the example of Eliot, "to arrange that the verse shall be intelligible even when the reference is not understood." But does Eliot's poem quite, or always, exhibit such tact? Once in later life, speaking about his allusions to the *Inferno*, Eliot said:

> I gave the references in my notes, in order to make the reader who recognized the allusion, know that I meant him to recognize it, and know that he would have missed the point if he did not recognize it.

That would imply that missing the reference to Dante really had damaged your understanding of the poetry, not just denied you some extra readerly pleasure – the recipe for a highly intellectualised sort of art; and Eliot was happy to entertain the thought that a reader should be prepared to put some solid effort into getting a poem: "it is to be expected that the reader of a poem should take at least as much trouble as a barrister reading an important decision on a complicated case".

At other times, however, Eliot suggests that poetry's mode of communication occurs on a whole other level, and that its 'meaning' (the sort of thing that one might piece together by recognising the allusions) is of secondary interest to the much stranger and deeper ways that poetry has of working:

The chief use of the "meaning" of a poem, in the ordinary sense, may be (for here I am speaking of some kinds of poetry and not all) to satisfy one habit of the reader, to keep his mind diverted and quiet, while the poem does its work upon him: much as the imaginary burglar is always provided with a bit of nice meat for the house-dog. This is a normal situation of which I approve.

One expression of this approach to poetic meaning was his conception of the "auditory imagination", which he characterised impressively:

the feeling for syllable and rhythm, penetrating far below the conscious levels of thought and feeling, invigorating every word; sinking to the most primitive and forgotten, returning to the origin and bringing something back, seeking the beginning and the end.

WHO IS SPEAKING?

The Victorian poet who probably mattered most to the young Eliot (as to his friend Pound) was Robert Browning, whose poetry was often written from behind the veil of a dramatis persona, as though excerpted from an unwritten play. J. Alfred Prufrock is a bit like a Browning character: the poem inhabits his skin, encouraging us at once to sympathise with him and to penetrate beneath his self-projection. The method

And elsewhere:

> I know that a poem, or a passage of a poem, may
> tend to realize itself first as a particular rhythm
> before it reaches expression in words, and that
> this rhythm may bring to birth the idea and the
> image.

"Poetry begins, I dare say," he told his audience at
Harvard, "with a savage beating a drum in the
jungle"; and part of that primitive or atavistic
appeal was its capacity, as though evading the
world of concepts, to "communicate before it is
understood". Worrying about the allusions you are
missing would, in that respect, be a distraction:
when it comes to reaching a readership, Eliot once
said, "it is the half-educated and ill-educated,
rather than the uneducated, who stand in his way",
adding, provocatively enough given that he was

of *The Waste Land* is related
to that, in that none of the
voices we hear is obviously or
unmistakeably that of
Thomas Stearns Eliot; but
the big poem is much less
coherently dramatised: it is
full of different characters
('He Do the Police in
Different Voices') but they
blend and merge into one
another unannounced. The
metaphor Eliot himself uses,
in his note about Tiresias in
Part III, is one of the poem's
multiple personae *melting*
into one another. The critic
Hugh Kenner has a good
phrase which captures the
way the poem is both the
expression of a coherent
sensibility and yet also an
assemblage of different
personalities: the poem
occupies, he says, a "zone of
consciousness" ▪

addressing an audience at Harvard: "I myself should like an audience which could neither read nor write."

It is unlikely that his listeners took offence at this declaration of preference, though Eliot was obviously not just joking. Still, it is difficult to see what an obliging reader might do to act upon his declared preference: since we can read and write, more or less, there is presumably nothing much to be done. Once there were critics who thought the essence of poetry lay in "pure sound"; but even they had to admit, as Empson judiciously observed, "that you have to be experienced in the words used by a poet before their sound can be appreciated, and evidently this admission makes all the difference".

No poem can communicate without *any* foreknowledge: if you respond to something in a language which you do not understand at all then you are responding to *something*, but not to the poem. As Eliot himself said, later in life, "the music of verse is inseparable from the meanings and associations of words"; and some of those associations are going to be from earlier appearances in literature. Allusiveness, in this very general sense, is just an aspect of the way literary language, and much ordinary language, always works; and that some of those associations are more specific than others appears simply a fact. (It would be hard to come across the word 'incarnadine' in a poem, for instance, without thinking of its inaugural appearance in *Macbeth*, or thinking that the poet meant you to be thinking of it.)

There is at stake here less a general principle about the propriety of assuming knowledge in your reader, and more a matter of tact about what it is polite or reasonable to assume the reader might recognise. Were you to read a brand new poem which referred with an air of knowingness to 'the waste land' and you *didn't* get the reference to T.S. Eliot's poem then something would be missing in your response, no doubt; and being encouraged to find something out about Eliot would be nothing but an improvement. Some of Eliot's references may seem *recherché* to most readers: not many have Sanskrit at their fingertips; but then Eliot helps with that in his own notes; and, as we shall see, there is a point to the very *alienness* that attaches to the poem's language when it approaches closest to spiritual hope.

To speak pragmatically, there are several excellent guides to the poem which will fill in the gaps as required (listed in the bibliography). And none of this is to say that other parts of the poem do not communicate much more directly, before any obvious labour has been expended. Eliot liked the idea of a Shakespeare play speaking to different bits of the Elizabethan audience on various 'levels' – from the simplest theatregoer who is merely enjoying the plot, through degrees of literary sophistication up to those "of greater sensitiveness and understanding", to whom "a meaning reveals itself gradually" – and, importantly, all this happens with no one in the house "bothered by the presence of that which he does not understand, or by the presence of that in which he is not interested". That feels like an idealised picture of a stratified society at ease with itself; but at least it implies the diverse kind of satisfaction that Eliot hoped his own poetry might be able simultaneously to achieve.

What is wrong with April?

1-18

So what is life as experienced in this 'zone'? The poem opens with a voice out of nowhere, purportedly the expression of some collective sort of experience (since it refers to 'us') and one which immediately defines itself through a deeply contrary attitude towards spring. Readers have often found coming to mind the opening line of the 'General Prologue' to Chaucer's *Canterbury Tales* – "Whan that Aprille with his shoures soote / The droghte of Marche hath perced to the roote..." ("When April with his sweet showers has pierced to the root the drought of March") – and a broad contrast between Eliot's lines and a whole set of inherited notions about the lovely virtues of April is obvious enough.

But the lines have a kind of intriguing imponderability about them all the same: "the first five words are a disagreement with – even a courteous rebuke to – something which it is believed that you sentimentally believe," says Christopher Ricks, though beyond that it is unclear just where the point of disagreement lies, something which becomes clear if you ponder just which of the words you should be stressing ("April"? "cruellest"?). Thus the poem opens, "decided in its uncertainty", in Gareth Reeves's phrase, from the off.

'The Burial of the Dead', the title of Part I, is what the Book of Common Prayer calls the funeral service, in the course of which the congregation is enjoined to the "sure and certain hope of the Resurrection to eternal life". But in this poem the new life brought by the returning spring is nothing but a curse: everything seems upside down here, where winter keeps you cosy and meddlesome April destroys things. This voice seems to be speaking on behalf ('us') of some mysterious all-but-dead people of some undisclosed legend, or at least people who had thought of themselves as practically dead and buried, just barely sustained within "[a] little life", a warm oblivion the loss of which they lament. The emergence of fresh vitality from this apparent death is regarded as a weary imposition: the lassitude of the rhymes (*breeding/mixing/stirring, covering/feeding*) conveys at best a flagging sort of half-life; and a sense of energies gone awry is further enforced by the straggle of those participles, each pinched off at the end of their lines by a comma, the run of their sentence repeatedly broken by enjambment.

Then, in the eighth line, in the first of the poem's many surprises of transition, a line about a surprise: "Summer surprised us, coming over the Starnbergersee". The referent of 'us' has silently shifted from the unwillingly revivified to the characters of a much more specific experience: by the sound of it, a contemporary European, staying in Munich (of which the Hofgarten is a public park and the Starnbergersee a nearby resort). The rain came as an unwelcome intervention to the speaker of the opening lines, and it disrupts life for our new speaker too, though on the more humdrum scale of being caught in a shower without a coat: the poem consistently works in this way, returning to re-imagine experience within new frames and contexts. A German speaks, perhaps the person who has ducked the shower: he says, as though alluding to the painful disorientations of nationality in contemporary Europe, "I am not at all Russian, I am from Lithuania – authentic German." (Lithuania exemplified the unhappy ambiguities of modern political identity: it had declared independence from the Russian Empire in 1918, resisting the attempts of the occupying Germans to retain it as a protectorate; and the country was soon resisting instead the invasive armies of the new Russian socialist state.)

The aristocratic female voice that marks the next transition has an unclear relationship with what has gone before, but her not thinking to explain who she is fits with the strange self-absorption of her childhood memory:

> *And when we were children, staying at the*
> *arch-duke's,*
> *My cousin's, he took me out on a sled,*
> *And I was frightened. He said, Marie,*
> *Marie, hold on tight. And down we went.*
> *In the mountains, there you feel free.*
> *I read, much of the night, and go south in the*
> *winter.*

People in the waste land almost all exist in this self-enclosed obliviousness. As it happens we know the real person on whom Eliot based this episode: she was called Countess Marie von Wallersee-Larisch; Eliot had met her, according to his widow, and he had also read her memoirs, which were entitled *My Past* (1913). But this is an example of a reference so private to Eliot's imaginative processes that its discovery cannot really be said to contribute much to the poem: it is precisely the unidentified nature of the voice that matters here. The lines brilliantly evoke the recollection of an intense, fearful, and covertly erotic pleasure, associated with a dangerous freedom that life has subsequently denied her; but the lines are not lachrymose: "I read, much of the night" is a tight-lipped brittle way of admitting to a besetting insomnia. The subsequent inconsequentiality of the conjunction "and go south in the winter" communicates a larger aimlessness in Marie's annual movements.

What is the waste land? *19-30*

And then we find ourselves abruptly in the "stony rubbish" of a waterless desert: "A heap of broken images", which many have taken to be a reference as well to the poem in which we find ourselves, presently a bit lost no doubt. At once solicitous and threatening, a prophetic voice (Eliot's notes point out the biblical parallels) invites us to find shelter from the heat; but he hardly offers much solace once we get there: "I will show you fear in a handful of dust." The Prayer Book order of service for the burial of the dead requires handfuls of earth to be cast upon the body while the priest intones, "Earth to earth, ashes to ashes, dust to dust"; but here no hope ensues. And, as Ricks has observed, the lines contain a moment of wonderfully judged grammatical dislocation that adds to the creation of menace:

Only
There is shadow under this red rock
(Come in under the shadow of this red rock),
And I will show you...

The Waste Land is not a consistently rhymed poem like 'The Rape of the Lock'; but, as we shall see, it is full of rhymes all the same; and full too, moreover, of broken approximations at rhyme (as in the opening lines). Here, there is a brilliantly inventive aridity involved in offering "this red rock" as a dead-rhyme with itself; and that paradoxical achievement is further enhanced by the syntax that encloses it. A sentence containing a bracket should make sense, grammatically, if the bracketed words are removed; but, as Ricks points out, that would not happen here, where "And I will show you" can make sense only if it can lean with confidence upon "Come in under the shadow of this red rock". But no such confidence is permitted here: the grammatical bewilderment of a parenthesis-which-is-no-parenthesis unsettles the voice, as though implying some distracting, unacknowledged trouble.

This verse drops us in a desert for the first time, the most obvious manifestation of the poem's governing idea of a 'waste land'. But what does that signify? Searching for the answer to that question has led many readers to the notes that Eliot supplied with the poem, the first one of which asserts:

> Not only the title, but the plan and a good deal of the incidental symbolism of the poem were suggested by Miss Jessie Weston's book on the Grail legend: *From Ritual to Romance*. Indeed, so deeply am I indebted, Miss Weston's book will elucidate the difficulties of the poem much better than my notes can do.

Many critics (Cleanth Brooks, for example, in a clever and influential essay) took him at his word and began with imagery found in Weston's book; and one of the things about his notes that Eliot came particularly to lament was the encouragement he had given to "a wild goose chase after Tarot cards and the Holy Grail". It is hard to believe that the Tarot pack which Madame Sosostris deploys in Part I can have detained many readers for long (Eliot's note makes disarmingly clear that he is dealing with a pack mostly of his own invention), but you could be forgiven for thinking the Holy Grail was a key element in the poem – even though, as Lawrence Rainey has pointed out, when Eliot first mentions the poem he has brewing, in a letter of November 1919, Weston's book is still to be published. (It appeared in January 1920.)

From Ritual to Romance is an analysis of the myths gathered around the Grail, a mysterious sacred object (a cup or a stone or a dish) which appears in Arthurian stories, and which became associated with the chalice used at Christ's Last Supper and with the vessel in which Joseph of Arimathea caught the blood that fell from Christ on the cross. This precious object was carelessly mislaid, and in many tales recovering the Grail becomes the object of a quest by Arthur's knights, Gawain or Perceval or Galahad, who set about their tasks in varying states of spiritual enlightenment. The important connection in the myth is that in achieving the Grail the successful quester simultaneously restores to fruitfulness a land that has long suffered from a dreadful drought: the waters are freed and the desert is irrigated once again.

In the legends associated with Perceval this waste land has a maimed and disabled king, the so-called 'Fisher King', presiding helplessly over the devastation; and it is his restoration to health that becomes the focus of the story. (This is the story that Wagner adopted for his opera *Parsifal*, which makes an appearance in *The Waste Land*.) Weston's theory was that, despite their trappings, these Grail stories had nothing to do with Christianity at all; that was a late piece of opportunism on the part of the medieval Church. No, what the Grail myths really represent are the lingering traces of fertility rites of unimaginable antiquity – "a prehistoric ritual possessing elements of extraordinary persistence and vitality," as Weston calls it, some occult spring ceremony undertaken to solicit the spirit of Vegetation to bring the water of life back to the land and to restore the impotent king of that waste land to wholeness once again.

Into her book Weston also weaves an explanation of the Tarot pack, originally used (she speculates) to predict the return of fertility to the land, as well as finding space in the theory for mumming plays, morris dancing, and much else besides.

What (almost but not quite, what *on earth*) did Eliot see in this esoteric grab-bag that spoke to the interests of his growing poem? Obviously, the myth provided a central metaphor: an arid landscape existing in symbolical relationship with a maimed and impotent human figure, a metaphor which it held within a narrative of possible redemption. But more generally, part of the appeal may have been its sheer reckless synthesising energy. Weston saw herself as writing in the wake of Sir James Frazer, a respectable figure though rarely consulted by anthropologists these days, whose monumental work *The Golden Bough* (originally 1890, with a third edition appearing in 1906-15) had, as Eliot said in the notes, "influenced our generation profoundly". Frazer's book gathered evidence from an immense range of folkloric traditions scattered across the world, not to emphasise the diversity of human experience but rather to discern within that wide variety the deep parallels that existed between the different mythologies, including Pagan and early Christian.

Weston took up that project with a new vehemence: her whole ambition is captured in one of her rhetorical questions – "Where shall we find a connecting link?" So long as folklorists only study little corners of the great subject, she says at one point, they will still be lacking "the skill of the most synthetic genius to co-ordinate them in one harmonious whole". Making connections between apparently irreconcilable elements, finding parallels between the experiences of modernity and those of ancient history, and co-ordinating all the fragments into a whole is what *The Waste Land* does too: Weston was by no means Eliot's only inspiration for his new kind of syncretic art, but her book appeared at the right moment to speak to his deepest compulsions. That is not to say that Eliot was wrong to discourage readers from chasing after the Grail: Ezra Pound, for one, was not persuaded that Weston helped much.

What does the German mean? *31-42*

We have had German once already in the poem (l.12) and now the language returns, but this time bringing with it for the first time an entire musical and spiritual world to which the poem will return. The voice is Richard Wagner's, an important influence on the texture of Eliot's poem, held together as it is by a large array of small recurrent devices – phrases, cadences, images, individual words. "The use of recurrent themes is as natural to poetry as to music," Eliot said in his later essay "The Music of Poetry"; and he must have had Wagner in mind, whose revolutionary music was known for what came to be known as 'leitmotifs', short, recurrent musical phrases each associated with a particular character or idea.

Eliot's early love of Wagner's operas was intense and highly emotional, and evidently formed an important part of the friendship he struck up during his time in Paris in 1910-11 with Jean

STRAVINSKY AND *THE WASTE LAND*

The main musical presence in the poem is undoubtedly Wagner, but another composer, a contemporary, also had an important role to play: Igor Stravinsky. Eliot attended performances of Diaghilev's ballets when the Ballets Russes visited London in the summer of 1921, and in a 'London Letter' contributed to *The Dial* (September 1921) he expressed his admiration for the way the ballets engaged with what's modern: the

Verdenal, a medical student with whom he lodged, whose death in the Great War affected Eliot deeply, and which he memorialised on the dedication page of *Prufrock and Other Observations* (1917). "I am beginning to get the hang of the *Ring*," he wrote to Verdenal in February 1912, implying a great dedication to the task; but another work evidently provoked a more spontaneous sort of excitement: "*Tristan and Isolde* is terribly moving at the first hearing, and leaves you prostrate with ecstasy and thirsting to get back to it again." You cannot imagine Eliot writing that way in English: liberatingly, he was writing to Verdenal in French; and when, years later, he discussed the opera with Stravinsky he was still able to leave the impression that *Tristan* was "one of the most passionate

effect of *La Boutique Fantasque* and *The Three-Cornered Hat,* he said, was "a simplification of current life"; but his greatest admiration was reserved for the ballets set to the music of Stravinsky, and especially *Le Sacre du Printemps* (*The Rite of Spring*) which, he said,

seem[s] to transform the rhythm of the steppes into the scream of the motor horn, the rattle of machinery, the grind of wheels, the beating of iron and steel, the roar of the underground railway, and the other barbaric cries of modern life; and to transform these despairing noises into music.

The mixture of ancient rite and the utterly up-to-date

experiences of his life".

The Ring of the Nibelung, Wagner's great opera cycle, will break into the poem in Part III; but for the moment, Eliot's thoughts are with *Tristan*. Based on a famous medieval story, Wagner's opera is one of the most rapturous portrayals of the power of erotic love. Tristan is a knight charged with bringing a reluctant Princess Isolde from Ireland to Cornwall, where she is to marry his master, King Mark; but on the boat the tragic pair drink a magic love potion and fall passionately for one another. Their love is doubly forbidden, by Tristan's normal loyalty to Mark and also by the obedience due to his crown; and yet it is irresistible. However, the consummation of their love in Act II is interrupted by Mark and his soldiers acting on a tip-off; Tristan is badly wounded; and the third and final act opens back in

was evidently inspiring for the poem in progress: "The spirit of the music was modern, and the spirit of the ballet was primitive ceremony."

There is another way in which Stravinsky's music might have helped to shape Eliot's audacious organisation of his material in *The Waste Land*. Like Eliot's poem, *The Rite of*

Spring declines to obey most of the customary musical rules: it cultivates all kinds of disharmony and sonic disarray, and resigns, in particular, the composer's classical duty to move music on from one theme to another through some kind of orderly transition between modes. For in Stravinsky's score, as Peter Hill has put it, the diverse elements appear

Brittany, with Tristan immobile and Kurwenal, his servant, looking forlornly out to sea for any sign of Isolde's approach. And she does come, but only to find Tristan already dead of his wound, a moment of bleak tragedy that Wagner magically conjures into ecstatic triumph: Isolde herself dies absorbed within a transfigurative vision of her Tristan risen again, and the opera ends with an extraordinary outpouring of celebratory *Liebestod* (love-death). Both lovers end up dead, true; but in Wagner's vision death, by removing them from the normal restraints and the circumspection of habitual morality, has merely freed their love for an ultimate consummation.

Now, the fragments of German embedded in *The Waste Land* are taken from Wagner's libretto, but they are chosen to imply an abruptly truncated version of the story. The four-line little song is the

to show a "total lack of reaction as one event follows another" – an effect that Hill memorably describes as a kind of anti-sentimentality, even "a reptilian indifference". Eliot's technique in *The Waste Land* shares some common ground with that, though it could hardly be said to endorse the "indifference" that it imagines so powerfully: the typist's "indifference" is a mark of sad disconnection. Such indifferent genius proved too much for those many members of Stravinsky's early audiences who greeted the performances with derisive laughter: according to Lyndall Gordon, Eliot sat among them, infuriated, poking the hooting philistines with the point of his umbrella ∎

first thing we hear in the opera after the overture, sung by a sailor on Tristan's boat: "Fresh blows the wind / To the homeland / My Irish child / Where do you dally?" The second fragment, a single line, comes from the very beginning of Act III, when the spirits of the opera are at their lowest and love seems to have been comprehensively defeated. Kurwenal asks if there is any sign of Isolde's approach and a shepherd bleakly replies: "The sea is empty and desolate." Eliot added that line to the typescript of the poem, thus brilliantly creating by implication a tragically reduced version of Wagner's exuberant love narrative: the poem is mindful of the triumph of love but only as a possibility it is not going to realise.

The German serves as a sort of frame to set another glimpsed anecdote: like the truncated *Tristan*, it is an episode in which some wonderful consummation is glimpsed but goes unrealised. The helpless speaker, faced with "the hyacinth girl", recalls his stumble into wordlessness:

> *I could not*
> *Speak, and my eyes failed, I was neither*
> *Living nor dead, and I knew nothing,*
> *Looking into the heart of light, the silence.*

The negatives stack up; but it is nicely poised whether this is a confession of emotional impotence, or a moment in which the poem, as Michael Edwards puts it, "seems to escape the toils of language, by looking to a possibility beyond speech". "Nothing" will resound through the poem, one of its main leitmotifs, pivoting on an uncertainty as to whether it nominates mere blank absence or some self-emptying state of possible enlightenment. For the time being, though, being "neither / Living nor dead" seems to locate this speaker squarely as an inhabitant of the unredeemed waste land, one who, to borrow a phrase from Hardy, is "the deadest thing / Alive enough to have strength to die". The "silence" into which he gazes, a Conradian darkness momentarily transfigured into luminous space, is no sooner introduced than it is absorbed back into the heartbroken silence of the empty sea, Isolde's ship nowhere in view.

What does Madame Sososotris foresee? *43-59*

If you stop believing in God, G.K. Chesterton is widely believed to have said, you do not start believing in nothing but rather in anything: whether that is true or not, Eliot was always attuned to the ways that an absence of faith led to credulity of the wrong kind. In his later poem 'The Dry Salvages' he enumerated some of the varieties of sub-religious experience:

> *spirits,*
> *To report the behaviour of the sea monster,*
> *Describe the horoscope, haruspicate or scry,*
> *Observe disease in signatures, evoke*
> *Biography from the wrinkles of the palm*
> *And tragedy from fingers...*

And on he lists:

> *all these are usual*
> *Pastimes and drugs, and features of the press:*
> *And always will be, some of them especially*
> *When there is distress of nations and perplexity*
> *Whether on the shores of Asia, or in the Edgware*
> *Road.*

Like those peddlers and practitioners of mystery, Madame Sosostris fulfils a felt need, but she is, as Gareth Reeves nicely puts it, "irresponsibly sibylline". She is a figure of spurious spiritual guidance, a so-so clairvoyante; but nevertheless, through her head cold, she approximately foresees the future of the poem: the drowned sailor (who will appear in Part IV), the Lady of the Rocks (whom we encounter shortly in Part II), the one-eyed merchant (who emerges in the unprepossessing shape of Mr Eugenides in Part III); and she advises us to fear death by water, a warning which will come good. Her inscrutability is strategic and financially advantageous ("Thank you"); and Eliot has the deft touch to insinuate her own vulnerability: "One must be so careful these days."

What happens on London Bridge? *60-76*

The diffuse sense of threat that Madame Sosostris feels is a product of living in London "these days". London is the "Unreal City" upon which the poem's camera has come to focus by the beginning of the last verse of Part I, and for much of the rest of the poem it will stay there. We have, for the first time, local landmarks mentioned by name: London Bridge, King William Street, St Mary Woolnoth (an early-18th century church on that street). It is a portrait of rush hour:

> *A crowd flowed over London Bridge, so many,*
> *I had not thought death had undone so many.*

"We have left undone those things which we ought to have done; And we have done those things which we ought not to have done" goes the general confession in the order for Evening Prayer.

   The poem returns to the thought of things undone, like the wind crossing "the brown land, unheard" in Part III, or the female voice later in the same section who laments: "Richmond and Kew / Undid me". Among the things the poem leaves undone so well is rhyme, and Christopher Ricks has analysed beautifully the dead-rhyme here:

> at once more richly a rhyme than any other could be, since it is the repetition of the very word itself, and yet more poverty-stricken than a *rhyme* could be, since it is not truly a rhyme at all, is not a creative cooperation of two things but instead has what is here the singleness of a consternation without parallel.

As though a parody of the water the loss of which the poem elsewhere regrets, it is the crowd that does the flowing here, and the prevailing fluent emptiness of purpose in the commuting traffic is nicely captured in Eliot's decision not to include a pronoun at all at l.67 ("Flowed up the hill and down King William Street") as though the attribution of particular agency were beside the point in such circumstances. The manuscript has one other striking effect in this part, one which Pound edited out: "To where St Mary Woolnoth kept the time / With a dead sound on the final stroke of nine." Eliot changed "time" to "hours", thus sadly removing the dead sound of his own

imperfect rhyme. ("A phenomenon which I have often noticed," read Eliot's deadpan note: this was his own walk to work.)

But a much more flamboyant piece of imagination is about to cross the poem's path. If Eliot's anthropological readings had encouraged him to seek out connections between the phenomena of modern life and those of days long dead, another spur was his absorption of James Joyce's novel *Ulysses*, the 'Circe' chapter of which he read in typescript in May 1921, and the complete text of which he subsequently reviewed. Eliot's first response to 'Circe', a night-time scene set in the brothel district, was to write a new opening for his poem set in low-life Boston: the first line of the greatest modern poem in English threatened for a time to become "First we had a couple of feelers down at Tom's place"; but that was not to make the final cut.

A more permanent effect of reading Joyce was highlighted in Eliot's review, where he singled out for praise the way that Joyce's novel was organised, with the events of contemporary Dublin mirroring in variously oblique ways the history of Odysseus: "In using the myth, in manipulating a continuous parallel between contemporaneity and antiquity," wrote Eliot, "Mr. Joyce is pursuing a method which others must pursue after him." Eliot attributed the viability of this new 'mythical method' to a number of modern influences, among them Frazer's anthropology, and we have already seen the way that Weston encouraged the finding of parallels between otherwise quite diverse kinds of historical experience, as though all human life were a series of metaphors for some fundamental and primitive reality. Joyce's example confirmed that interest powerfully, and while *The Waste Land* does not operate "a continuous parallel", it does bring "contemporaneity and antiquity" into a tandem relationship repeatedly.

The startling inauguration of this art of double-perspective comes on London Bridge. The verse reads like a surreal translation of an encounter in Dante's underworld:

> *There I saw one I knew, and stopped him crying:*
> *'Stetson!*
> *'You who were with me in the ships at Mylae!*
> *That corpse you planted last year in your garden,*
> *Has it begun to sprout?*

Mylae was a famous battle in the Punic Wars fought between Rome and Carthage, in which the Romans were victorious: it is the first of several glimpses of Carthage, implying a parallel between the recent horrors of Europe and the calamities of antiquity. The speaker's grisly questions return to the perversions of fertility with which the poem began, heightened now by the unhinged incongruity of asking such crazy things of an old lag from your time in the forces whom you spot while walking to work. What could be more normally English than a chat about gardening? But Eliot repeatedly finds things that disturb lurking deep beneath the dulled shapes of the reassuringly ordinary. 'The Burial of the Dead' is partly about things that won't stay buried, such as corpses and desires and memories; and if we are tempted to regard all this with a sympathetic but clinical disinterest then the last line, taken from Baudelaire, would persuade us otherwise: "You! Hypocrite reader! My fellow man! My brother!"

Who are these women? 77–172

We are now firmly in London, and Part II consists of two portraits of women from different parts of the city and opposite ends of the social scale. It opens with the 'mythical method' firmly in mind: this lady – presumably "Belladonna, the Lady of the Rocks, / The lady of situations" whom Madame Sosostris foresaw – is held in parallel with Shakespeare's Cleopatra. Here Pound's attentions worked a wonder. The typescript he received opened its second part with these lines:

> The Chair she sat in, like a burnished throne
> Glowed on the marble, where the swinging glass
> Held up by standards wrought with golden vines

"3 lines. Too tum-pum at a stretch," wrote Pound in his inimitable marginal manner. Which is to say, he thought three lines too many for Eliot to stay within the regular iambic pentameter of his source, Enobarbus's marvelling speech about the Egyptian Queen in *Antony and Cleopatra*:

> The barge she sat in, like a burnish'd throne
> Burned on the water: the poop was beaten gold;
> Purple the sails, and so perfumed that
> The winds were lovesick with them... (II.ii)

Eliot listened and produced this small but decisive change:

> *The Chair she sat in, like a burnished throne,*
> *Glowed on the marble, where the glass*
> *Held up by standards wrought with fruited vines...*

The second line comes in a foot short, a piece of dark metrical wit that conveys a modern state of mind fully conscious of Cleopatra's sexy magnificence but falling just short of realising it. The effect leans towards a kind of serious mock-heroic, in which a diminished present is contrasted with the largeness and reach of the past: for "barge" read "chair". That is, our reading experience should really be: "The ~~barge~~ Chair she sat in, like a burnished throne". As Cleopatra's royal boat proceeds along the river, the breezes

TEN RESPONSES TO *THE WASTE LAND*

1.
Shortly after the publication of the poem Pound wrote: "Eliot's *Waste Land* is I think the justification of the 'movement', of our modern experiment, since 1900."

2.
Asked her view, the American poet and collector Amy Lowell said: "I think it is a piece of tripe."

3.
W.B. Yeats was a highly qualified admirer: "Eliot has produced his great effect upon his generation because he has described men and women that get out of bed or into it from mere habit; in describing this life that has lost heart his own art seems grey, cold, dry... in *The Waste Land*, amid much that is moving in symbol and imagery there is much monotony of accent:

> When lovely woman stoops to folly and
> Paces about her room again, alone,
> She smooths her hair with automatic hand,
> And puts a record on the gramophone.

I was affected, as I am by these lines, when I saw for the first time a painting by Manet. I longed for the vivid colour and light of Rousseau and Courbet, I could not endure the grey middle-tint..."

4.

Eliot's contemporary James Joyce, an influence upon *The Waste Land*, was also an admirer of it. After reading the poem he remarked to a friend: "I had never realized Eliot was a poet." When his friend replied, "I liked it too but I couldn't understand it," Joyce answered: "Do you have to understand it?" Later he wrote a skit on it for his patron ("Rouen is the rainiest place").

5.

Conrad Aiken, Eliot's Harvard contemporary, wrote a review of the poem which he entitled "An Anatomy of Melancholy", a piece of news he passed on to Eliot. "He turned on me," Aiken recalled, "with that icy fury of which he alone was capable, and said fiercely, 'There is nothing melancholy about it!' To which I in turn replied: 'The reference, Tom, was to BURTON's *Anatomy of Melancholy*, and the quite extraordinary amount of *quotation* it contains!' The joke was acceptable, and we both roared with laughter."

6.

The aesthete Harold Acton, while a student at Oxford, declaimed passages from the poem from the balcony of his set in Christ Church. In the

Oxford episode of Evelyn Waugh's *Brideshead Revisited* (1945) Anthony Blanche, deploying a megaphone, "in languishing tones recited passages from *The Waste Land* to the sweatered and muffled throng that was on its way to the river". Waugh entitled one of his other novels *A Handful of Dust* (1934).

7.

The politician Tom Driberg, also a student at Christ Church, was a friend of W.H Auden. "[O]nly a few years ago," Driberg recalled towards the end of his life, "he gave me a copy of one of this books inscribed 'To Tom Driberg, who made me read *The Waste Land*'. His recollection was correct: we read this truly epoch-making poem for the first time together: read it, standing side by side in my rooms, in a copy of the first issue of Eliot's review, *The Criterion*; read it, at first, with incredulous hilarity (the Mrs Porter bit, for instance); read it, again and again, with growing awe."

8.

The black American writer Ralph Ellison remembered encountering the poem in his reading at college:

> *Wuthering Heights* had caused me an agony of unexpressible emotion, and the same was true of *Jude the Obscure*, but *The Waste Land* seized my mind. I was intrigued by its power to move me

while eluding my understanding. Somehow its rhythms were often closer to those of jazz than those of the Negro poets, and even though I could not understand then, its range of allusion was as mixed and as varied as that of Louis Armstrong. Yet there were its discontinuities, its changes of pace and its hidden system of organization which escaped me.

There was nothing to do but look up the references in the footnotes to the poem, and thus began my conscious education in literature.

9.

Ted Hughes revered Eliot, and was struck by the way that "this immensely learned, profound, comprehensive, allusive masterpiece is also a popular poem" ('The Song of Songs in the Valley of Bones'). Eliot, towards the end of his life, had become the young Hughes's publisher at Faber and Faber. In an early letter, Hughes had written to thank him for something, and signed off: "I hope you are well, and enjoying April." Eliot's response is not known.

10.

Wendy Cope wittily reduces the poem to five 'Waste Land Limericks' in her volume, *Making Cocoa for Kingsley Amis* (1986), which was published by Eliot's own firm, Faber and Faber.

and the water fall in love with her; but this new Cleopatra occupies a claustrophobic place, "the room enclosed", full of pungent artificial perfumes mixed with heavy smoke from the fire, the atmosphere less "lovesick" than just plain sick and in need of a breath of fresh air:

> *her strange synthetic perfumes,*
> *Unguent, powdered, or liquid – troubled, confused*
> *And drowned the sense in odours; stirred by the air*
> *That freshened from the window, these ascended...*

Grammatical sense gets drowned in this place too: in *Seven Types of Ambiguity* Empson described the way the language moves queasily between grammatical possibilities, so that here, for instance, "troubled, confused" come before you as adjectives (on the model of "powdered") only to tremble belatedly into verbs – a shift of perspective

VIVIEN ELIOT IN
THE WASTE LAND

The connection between the poem and the unhappiness of the Eliots' marriage has long been the subject of speculation; and Vivien evidently played an important role in the making of the poem. When in October 1921 Eliot headed for Margate to undergo a medical regime for his nerves, as well as to put his mind to the poem long contemplated, he was clear that he wanted

that "gives a sense of swooning or squinting", Empson says finely.

This section of the poem is entitled 'A Game of Chess', which is a quotation from it (137), as well as being, as Eliot notes, an allusion to the title of a play by Middleton, in which the moves of a chess game are staged in parallel to a forced seduction. The lines glimpse the possibilities of love in heroic measure but only to show its diminishment or disappointment: the "golden Cupidon" (80) is not the agent of Venus but a coy piece of baroque titillation; and the pretentious decoration suggested by "laquearia" (92), which is merely a panelled ceiling, folds into the poetry by allusion a reference to the palace of Dido, Queen of Carthage (as described by Virgil), whose heart is broken when she is deserted by her lover, Aeneas.

There is more classical cruelty, and sexual violence, in the shadows: in the "sad light" of the

Vivien to come with him:

I am supposed to be alone, but I could [not] bear the idea of starting this treatment quite alone in a strange place, and I have asked my wife to come with me and stay with me as long as she is willing.

Theirs was a troubled

marriage, certainly, but the letters of the time give the impression of a couple who felt themselves bound, in a way, by their troubles, especially by their sharing of anxieties about health, which were largely worries about how they were damaging one another. "I hope that I shall place less strain upon Vivien," he wrote to his lady's room we discover a painting, a "sylvan scene", which sounds banal enough until you pick up the reference to which Eliot alerts us, and find this is Satan's view of the Garden of Eden as he approaches "delicious Paradise" intent on destroying the innocence of its inhabitants. The subject painted in this picture is also terrible: "The change of Philomel, by the barbarous king / So rudely forced". Pound seems to have been doubtful about these lines, writing "1921" in the margin, a sign that he thought Eliot was ducking out of the duty to be modern; but the euphemistic quality of the description ("rudely") is intended purposefully to imply some basic wrongness in attitude, and Eliot kept his original wording.

It certainly doesn't sound a very good picture; a tame piece of cod-classicism; but lurking within it is one of the most appalling stories of antiquity, which Eliot takes from Ovid's *Metamorphoses*. In

brother in December 1921, "who has to do so much *thinking* for me."

The phrase catches an unexpected resemblance with lines that Eliot had written not long before for the lady in Part II, whom many have thought to be modelled on Vivien: "What are you thinking of? What thinking? What? / I never know what you are thinking. Think." That sort of passing entanglement of life and poem is striking; and, generally, what can be pieced together of her role in the making of the poem is intriguing, a testimony to the mysterious workings of marriage.

Eliot evidently placed some value on Vivien's

it, King Tereus rapes Philomela (Eliot prefers the form "Philomel") and cuts out her tongue; but by weaving a tapestry she communicates the nature of the crime to her sister, who is the queen, who in turn takes revenge on Tereus by killing their son and serving him up as dinner. The Ovidian story closes this grotesque tale with a magical metamorphosis of the three characters into birds, which is what the picture must be depicting, the "change" of Philomela into a nightingale whose "inviolable voice" Eliot imagines filling "all the desert": "And still she cried, and still the world pursues, / "Jug Jug" to dirty ears" – "Jug Jug" being a representation of birdsong in Elizabethan poetry but also a crude term for sex (the smutty double entendre is picked up by "dirty ears").

Her voice emerges from a dreadful violation, which it transforms into a voice that can no longer be violated; but you feel that that the hard-won

judgments: for instance, once he had put a rough draft of Part III together, in November 1921, he waited on her advice before going on, needing "Vivien's opinion as to whether it is printable"; and Vivien clearly went through at least some of the manuscript for she left her comments on Part II. "Don't see what you had in mind here," she writes sideways next to the description of the modern Cleopatra; but when Eliot turns the verse to dialogue her pencil turns to capitals of praise: "WONDERFUL"; then "Yes", "& wonderful", "wonderful". She makes a suggested change to "The hot water at ten", putting a caret after "hot" and writing

"bottle!" The suggestion maybe reflects a habitual detail of their life: "It seems to me an achievement," Vivien wrote admiringly about Eliot's periodical *The Criterion* to Sydney Schiff, a novelist and patron of the arts, "by a man who has only his evenings, tired out by eight hours in the City, and who fills hot water bottles, and makes invalid food for his wretchedly unhealthy wife, in between writing!"

Perhaps a similarly personal reference, but this time too close to the bone of their unhappy domesticity,

T.S. Eliot and Vivien, circa 1920

lies behind the decision to cut the line about the chessmen – "The ivory men make company between us" – which was omitted, according to Valerie Eliot, "at Vivien Eliot's request". (Eliot replaced the line when he made a copy of the poem towards the end of his life.)

The last part of Part II, about Lil and Albert, was based, Eliot later recalled, on their maid, Ellen Kellond; and here Vivien, who evidently shared Eliot's regard for her anecdotes, had several suggestions to make. Her pencil changed "Something of" to purity of that cry goes unheard in this dressing room. The atrocity that befalls Philomela is accompanied by other art works and *objets*, "withered stumps of time", as though the backdrop to the strange, cosmetic, chemical life of the lady were a low hum of imperfectly aestheticised, perpetual suffering. Philomela "still" cries and "still the world pursues": beneath the veneer of classical cultivation, something lies "savagely still".

"Why do you never speak. Speak": what ensues is the most remarkable non-conversation in English poetry. The lady's words are in inverted commas, so presumably uttered aloud; and her non-interlocutor's (let's say, her husband's) lack them, so presumably they remain within his mind; but the line between what's inside and what's outside is never easy firmly to establish in this poem. Her speech is insistent, pitiable, needy, exasperating; his silence is no less persecutory.

"somethink o'", a closer approximation to Ellen's voice; "I want to avoid trying [to] show pronunciation by spelling," wrote Eliot in response. But other proposals were adopted. "If you dont like it you can get on with it", presumably a piece of Ellen-speak, Eliot took up and made into l.153. The bleak documentary detail of the "pills" is Vivien's (l.159): Eliot originally had "medicine". And the terrible line, "What you get married for if you don't want children?" (l.164) grew from Vivien's suggested replacement for "You want to keep him at home I suppose": "What you get married for if you dont want to have children?" "Splendid last

Pound evidently thought the passage simply too close to being a transcription of her neurotic remarks: "photography", he wrote on the manuscript, not intending praise; but Vivien, Eliot's wife, whom many have taken to be the model, also commented on the passage and wrote "wonderful". It is much more than "photography", of course, because, while entirely convincing in its own dramatic terms, the apparent accidentals of what the lady happens to say all take their part within the larger orchestration of the poem. One of the poem's most insistent keynotes recurs:

'What is that noise now? What is the wind doing?
Nothing again nothing.
'Do
'You know nothing? Do you see nothing? Do you remember
'Nothing?'

lines," she adds at the bottom, by Ophelia's curtain line; and on the other of the sheet: "Make any of these alterations — or none if you prefer. Send me back this copy & let me have it".

When the poem appeared in the first number of *The Criterion*, Vivien's response was overpowering: "Perhaps not even you can imagine with what emotions I saw *The Waste Land* go out into the world," she wrote to Schiff, who praised the poem: "It means to me a great deal of what you have exactly described, and it has become a part of me (or I of it) this last year. It was a terrible thing, somehow, when the time came at last for it to be published." ∎

The rapt failure in the hyacinth garden, in which the speaker "knew nothing" and "could not / Speak", is here recast in a darker, accusatory key. What he does remember ("Those are pearls that were his eyes") has all the inexplicable vividness of a traumatic private memory; but it is also a line from Shakespeare's *The Tempest*, sung by Ariel, describing the "sea-change" he imagines happening to the body of the king, whom he pretends is drowned at the bottom of the sea; and it is also a memory of Eliot's own poem, for this Shakespearean line has already been uttered with a strangely imperative force by Madame Sosostris (l.48).

The poem keeps remembering itself this way, repeatedly turning over little scraps of language to which pressing but unspecified emotions have become attached, as though recollecting oneself might be a way of pulling oneself together. Eliot thus exemplifies the profound wisdom enunciated by Wordsworth, who once observed that "every man must know that an attempt is rarely made to communicate impassioned feelings without something of an accompanying consciousness of the inadequateness of our own powers, or the deficiencies of language"; and in such circumstances, as he went on, "there will be a craving in the mind, and as long as it is unsatisfied the Speaker will cling to these same words, or words of the same character".

Vivien Eliot, London, 1921

With nothing to cling to, clinging to words is what this lady does, and among other things that means clinging to "nothing": "Is there nothing in your head?"

> But
> *O O O O that Shakespeherian Rag—*
> *It's so elegant*
> *So intelligent*

Eliot shares with Joyce an interest in the trivial things that (as we say) come to mind through the

association of ideas, things at once prompted
and pointless: in this case, a scrap from a ragtime
song, half-remembered – the original goes
"That Shakespearian rag, / Most intelligent,
very elegant". The jollity of the song comes across
as horribly sardonic in the setting, its private
invocation a kind of inner defence against his
wife's pressing unhappiness; but *The Waste Land*
is indeed woven from many rags, Shakespearean
and otherwise, and Eliot is simultaneously saying
something knowing and self-deprecating about his
own poem's technique. There are several moments
in the poem, as we have begun to see, where Eliot
finds a self-reflective resonance in words that are
also engaged properly on their own business.

The Shakespearean rag comes to mind because
The Tempest has just come to mind, but also,
perhaps, because, after his wife's demands that he
"speak", her repetition of "nothing" has prompted
thoughts of *King Lear*, a play through which that
null word rings. Shakespeare's king peremptorily
demands speeches of love from his daughters, the
youngest of whom, like the *Waste Land* husband,
stubbornly refuses to play this needy game:

LEAR
   ... what can you say to draw
   A third more opulent than your sisters? Speak.
CORDELIA
   Nothing, my lord.

LEAR
    Nothing!
CORDELIA
    Nothing.
LEAR
    Nothing will come of nothing: speak again.

And the tragedy goes on to play out the inevitability of Lear's unwitting prophecy. Nothing to be done for our couple either: to wait for the hot water, to look forward to the taxi ordered for four, and meanwhile to play "a game of chess". "The ivory men make company between us", a line in manuscript which Eliot removed, was restored when he made a transcription of the complete poem in 1960, and it deserves its place: a sudden odd tenderness lifts the phrase – the poignancy that, in the absence of anything genuinely companionable, this temporary forging of a connection is at least something – and implies a fuller range of emotions at work in this marital attrition.

    With an abrupt cut, we are in an East End pub, approaching closing time, some time after the Armistice of 1918 and the coming home of the troops. The couple in the first section of Part II appear childless; having children is part of the horror for the couple described in the second. Her body undermined by chemically induced miscarriage ("them pills"), Lil is advised by her intrusive but possibly well-meaning friend to make herself "a bit smart" and to equip herself with new false teeth, all of which is intended to retain the sexual interest of her returning soldier-husband. "And if you don't give it him, there's others will," the garrulous speaker tells Lil: "You ought to be ashamed, I said, to look so antique." (That has a mordant sort of wit about it, as Craig Raine observes, given that a resemblance to what's "antique" lies at the heart of Eliot's 'mythical method'.)

"HURRY UP PLEASE IT'S TIME", says the pub landlord with repeated insistence to these victims of time, not deploying the standard follow-up cry of the profession: "Ain't you got homes to go to?" Not much of a home here, if home is where the heart is; but still, there is a flash of companionship in the hot gammon, the "beauty" of which Lil and Albert share with their gossipy friend – the one time the word "beauty" appears in the poem. As they drunkenly say goodnight to one another, their London voices merge into the death speech of Ophelia: "Good night, ladies, good night, sweet ladies, good night, good night." Part II has begun mindful of one of Shakespeare's tragic heroines and ends quoting another; but if the opening lines allowed an edge of bathos about the comparison it was drawing between the old Cleopatra and the new, then this closing parallel seems anything but mocking: there feels no disparity in the levels of tragedy being played out at the opposite ends of literary history. Ophelia utters her words before she goes off to drown; and it is with a river that the next section begins.

What is the Fire Sermon?
173-214

This section is entitled 'The Fire Sermon', named after a sermon given by the Buddha to warn his followers of the consuming powers of human passion.

> All things, O priests, are on fire... The eye, O priests, is on fire; forms are on fire; eye-consciousness is on fire; impressions received by the eye are on fire; and whatever sensation, pleasant, unpleasant, or indifferent, originates in dependence on impressions received by the eye, that also is on fire.

Only by acquiring a scrupulous obliviousness toward these things is a person able to attain freedom from the omnipresent and tortuous depravity that otherwise characterises the bodily life. Buddhism may enter the poem from a number of directions: Eliot had studied it at Harvard in 1912 (he refers to his text book, Henry Clarke Warren's *Buddhism in Translation* – properly

'Translations' – in his note to l.308); and his interest may have been further kindled by Wagner's engagement with the religion, in turn the result of his reading in the philosopher Schopenhauer: clear traces of his Buddhist preoccupations get into *Parsifal*. Evidently, Eliot was intuitively drawn to the renunciatory temper of Buddhism, though in this part of the poem he deftly intertwines Buddhist and Christian conceptions of fire together in an idiosyncratically synthetic way to make something new of both.

The waste land in which we found ourselves in Part I lacked water ("the dry stone no sound of water"); and as 'The Fire Sermon' begins we finally have some; but, in one of the many dark ironies of juxtaposition that the poem increasingly deploys, it brings no relief. Bracing themselves against the Elizabethan charm of Spenser's line, "Sweet Thames, run softly, till I end my song", Eliot's opening lines depict a squalid urban river, a scene of autumnal decay to which Eliot gives in passing an almost Gothic *frisson*: "the last fingers of leaf / Clutch and sink into the wet bank". The lovely Spenser line comes from his 'Prothalamion', a poem written to celebrate both a particular marriage (in fact, two) as well as marriage in general: it might promise to be a bruising sort of prologue to the bleak scene of seduction that forms the centrepiece of both Part III and, as Eliot's note tells us, the poem as a whole; but the temper of the lines is elegiac and sorry, as though a whole tradition of poetry were coming to an end.

As elsewhere in the poem, the London facts fit with a wonderfully pitched unease and disease among the inherited conventions of the English lyric:

> *The nymphs are departed.*
> *And their friends, the loitering heirs of city*
> *directors –*
> *Departed, have left no addresses.*

Eliot wrote bits of the poem while convalescing on Lake Leman (the French name for Lake Geneva) so part of the reference in "By the waters of Leman I sat down and wept..." must be private; but the cadence is biblical, the lament of the exiled Israelites ("By the waters of Babylon we sat down and wept: when we remembered thee, O Sion" (Psalm 137)), and there is a further twist that fits with the depleted sexiness of the autumnal Thames in that "leman" is also an archaically literary word for a sweetheart or a lover. Spenser uses it in *The Faerie Queene*: "He... offred kingdoms vnto her in vew, / To be his Leman and his Lady trew". In a few lines' time we will hear of another who weeps by his watery lover (297-8).

The Spenserian Thames is soon downgraded to "the dull canal". The poem continues to interweave glimpses of up-to-date urban

modernity ("round behind the gashouse")
with fragments of an older style, now returning to
an odd mangle of Shakespeare's *The Tempest*
– Ferdinand thinks his father dead, "Sitting on a
bank, / Weeping again the king my father's wrack"
(I.ii), where Eliot's lines curiously invent a new
sibling, "the king my brother's wreck / And on the
king my father's death before him" – and now
updating Andrew Marvell's 'Coy Mistress' for the
machine age. Marvell had the lovely elegance of
"But at my back I always hear / Time's wingèd
chariot hurrying near", which gets roughened into
contemporaneity as "But at my back from time to
time I hear / The sound of horns and motors,
which shall bring / Sweeney to Mrs. Porter in the
spring". Mrs Porter, who sounds a colourful lady,
then becomes the subject of a song that one might
have guessed was bawdy even if scholarship had
not subsequently confirmed the point; and then
the verse jags into a line of soaring French which,
Eliot's notes informs us, comes from Verlaine's
Wagnerian sonnet 'Parsifal'.

The juxtapositions here are pretty stark and
ugly: the sonnet describes the knight Parsifal
having overcome the fleshly temptations, healed
the maimed king of the legend, and finally come
face to face with the Grail itself, at which point of
giddy spiritual elevation the children burst into
celebratory, innocent song (as they do, indeed, at
the end of Act I of Wagner's opera): "And O the

voice of those children singing in the cupola!" The tone of this part of the poem seems bitterly erratic, uncaring, as though the emotions of the poem were veering dangerously towards some breaking point; the idiom shifts crazily from demotic to mandarin and back again; and finally it descends into what looks like nonsense:

> *Twit twit twit*
> *Jug jug jug jug jug jug*
> *So rudely forc'd.*
> *Tereu*

This is a farrago of things from the story of Philomela, imprecisely mediated through a painful memory: a nice touch, especially, that "so rudely forced" should reappear archaically as "so rudely forc'd", in a poem that remembers and half-remembers old things so persistently. What might have seemed the natural beauty of birdsong, innocent as the children in Parsifal's cupola, is now ghosted by a sexual violence that we might not have suspected once but cannot now entirely forget: "After such knowledge," as Eliot wrote elsewhere, "what forgiveness?" "Tereu", says B.C. Southam, is the vocative form of 'Tereus': that is, the form of his name you would use if you were addressing him, or crying out to him.

The vehement and uncertainly angry spirit that stirs in some of these transitions may be a hangover from the long original opening to Part III, which Pound cut out in its entirety and which the verse beginning "The river's tent is broken" was drafted late on in the composition history to replace. Those original lines contained the portrait of another London lady, cast very broadly in the satirical Augustan manner of Alexander Pope's *The Rape of the Lock*. The lady under threat this time is fashionable 'Fresca', who is admittedly a tiresome knucklehead, with a superficial interest in books and conversation and what the critics say; but the level of contumely on display feels out of proportion to her failings, and the decision of Pound (who was ready enough himself to rise to contumely when the age demanded) was undoubtedly right.

The disgust at Fresca's smell, and the withering description of her type as "Unreal emotions, and real appetite" is startling; but while the emotions in play are real all right, it is hard not to feel that the poetry misses that criterion of intelligence which Eliot elsewhere offered in a more even temper: "the discernment of exactly what, and how much, we feel in any given situation". "Fresca was baptised in a soapy sea / Of Symonds–Walter Pater–Vernon Lee", writers of whom Eliot disapproved; but I hope there are worse things in the moral universe than reading the wrong authors and talking pretentiously about them. Elsewhere there is an odd uncertainty of aim even in the literary satire: Fresca originally reads "a page of Gibbon" while having her lazy breakfast in bed, which Eliot changed in typescript to "the Daily Mirror", a rather different order of cultural faux pas one would have thought. Eliot obeyed Pound's instructions to cut the whole passage, recalling his brusque guidance a few years later:

> Pope has done this so well that you cannot do it better; and if you mean this as a burlesque, you had better suppress it, for you cannot parody Pope unless you can write better verse than Pope - and you can't.

Anyway, much more effective is the imponderable blank tone in which we learn about Mr Eugenides, a merchant from Smyrna, who propositions the speaker (whoever the speaker is by now) with an invitation to Brighton: his "pocket full of currants" is a superb novelistic touch, which inclines towards his double, the drowned Phoenician sailor in Part IV. Plausibly, I think, Eliot reportedly declared himself unconscious of any specific homosexual implication: for the feeling of the lines is genuinely nonplussed, not knowing quite *what* is going on. (Who is to say the speaker at this point is not a woman?) There followed then in manuscript another passage of angry moral denunciation – "London, your people is bound upon the wheel! / Phantasmal gnomes ... aberrant from the normal equipoise" – which Pound sensibly excised with the tart comment "B*ll***s"; but Eliot recovered something like his own "equipoise" to embark on what he thought of himself as the central episode of the work.

What does Tiresias see?
215-265

"Tiresias, although a mere spectator and not indeed a 'character', is yet the most important personage in the poem, uniting all the rest... What Tiresias *sees*, in fact, is the substance of the poem," says Eliot in his note to l.218. Tiresias in the Greek myth (Eliot's note quotes the version by Ovid) is one of those victims of the gods behaving badly. He happened to have experienced life both as a man and as a woman (hence the references to his "wrinkled female breasts" and "dugs"), and consequently found himself called in to settle a disagreement between Jove and Juno about which partner derived most pleasure from sex. Tiresias supported Jove's contention that it was women who enjoyed it more, for which answer Juno crossly blinded him; and Jove granted him long life and the gift of prophecy as a consolation for his lost sight. Disputed claims to sexual pleasure are forlornly irrelevant to the encounter between the typist and the clerk, of course; what Eliot's

Tiresias is really expert in is the profound unsatisfactoriness felt on both sides, and he bleakly regards the act he witnesses as exemplary: "And I Tiresias have foresuffered all / Enacted on this same divan or bed".

Pound's intervention here was brilliant. Eliot originally cast the account in quatrains (ABAB), but Pound cut out lines and phrases without any reference to the verse form he was mauling: "verse not interesting enough as verse to warrant so much of it," he wrote on the manuscript. Enough of the quatrain pattern survives for it to linger in the ear as a ghost, but the reality that meets us is much less orderly, with broken lines, lost grammar, and unrhymed endings, beautifully enacting the sense of human dislocation that hangs over the whole episode. The time is "the violet hour", we are told twice, a colour that will recur in the poem: that is, twilight, but, now that our inner-ears have been sensitised by the description of Philomela's "inviolable voice", with a glancing pun on "violate". Lovely lines of Sappho, which address the evening star as the daily inspiration for homecoming, are given a sad twist:

> ...the evening hour that strives
> Homeward, and brings the sailor home from sea,
> The typist home at teatime, clears her breakfast, lights
> Her stove, and lays out food in tins.

This is the other end of the working day: the typist loses the subject pronoun we look to find ('she') just as the commuters walking to work in Part I had lost theirs. Pound judiciously cut back some of the satirical disgust that he found in the lines: her tins originally contained "squalid food", and a little later Tiresias had declared himself expert in "the manner of these crawling bugs" – "Too easy," wrote Pound, correctly. The result of their collaboration was to release the powerful sympathy that had always stirred in the lines alongside Eliot's moral exasperation.

> *The time is now propitious, as he guesses,*
> *The meal is ended, she is bored and tired,*
> *Endeavours to engage her in caresses*
> *Which still are unreproved, if undesired.*

"Still" discovers another resonance with Philomela ("And still she cried, and still the world pursues"): as there, it hovers between "nevertheless" and (more bleakly) something like "as is always the way". Moral decision has been reduced to a gathering of negations, actions undone and emotions unfelt: the agent has become a "human engine" like a taxi (one was ordered in Part II); and the typist is reduced to the automatism of the gramophone she operates.

The house agent's clerk is a thorough adept in the world of non-connection: "His vanity requires no response, / And makes a welcome of indifference." There is some sharply unforgiving play here with the great lines of chastened consolation that end Samuel Johnson's 'Vanity of Human Wishes': hope may be doomed, but love, patience, and faith yet remain, says Johnson, and "With these celestial Wisdom calms the Mind, / And makes the happiness she does not find." But there is nothing of such wisdom here, and the aftermath of the event is not even dismay or disgust but numbness, the very opposite of reflection, as the typist continues still to exist at one remove from her own life – "Her brain allows one half-formed thought to pass" is about as far from "she thought" as the language can get. The ending of the section is a miracle of tone: Eliot manages to invoke a lovely sad song from Goldsmith ("When lovely woman stoops to folly / And finds too late that men betray") in a way which rejects its sentimental moralism without jettisoning its pathos. As Ricks and Reeves notice, a lot hangs on the placing of the word *and*:

> *When lovely woman stoops to folly and*
> *Paces about her room again, alone,*
> *She smoothes her hair with automatic hand,*
> *And puts a record on the gramophone.*

The small removal of "and" from the second line sends Goldsmith's line off-kilter by adding an extra foot. It makes a mockery of the lesson so consequentially learned about "men" in the original: the new "and" receives a very heavy emphasis (as Eliot makes clear in his own recording of the poem) but moving on to see what this "and" entails in the next line reveals only a deepening sense of aimlessness. Much of the pity lies in the devastating placement of those commas in l.254 and the weight they throw on the isolated word, "alone" – an emphasis which brings into play the word's other appearance, in a different context of sexual predation: "Well, if Albert won't leave you alone, there it is, I said". "[S]o all the women are one woman", Eliot's note advises.

The music from the gramophone is heard by someone outside, perhaps; or maybe another voice within this zone of consciousness is recalling the line from *The Tempest* that follows the passage half-remembered at l.191. The song of the children, celebrating the end of Parsifal's Buddhist-like quest to overcome desire, is now answered by another tune, coming from a pub near the fish market: that seems an unlikely source for purity, but the tune is apparently overheard from the church of St Magnus Martyr, and suddenly a flash of light appears in this very dark place – "Inexplicable splendour of Ionian white and gold." The inexplicability is like the incommunicability experienced in the hyacinth garden, poised undecidably between something wondrously inexpressible and something that's just bewildering.

What do the Thames maidens sing? *266-311*

The spirits of the poem are beginning to seem depleted, as though it has been through the extremes of experience: the lines are shortening, out of breath, out of eloquence, taciturn. Two verses sketch a contrast between the Thames now and the Thames of Elizabeth: the first polluted, industrial, mercantile; the second regal, golden, and musical, an emulation of the lavish barge of Cleopatra glimpsed between the lines in Part II. The contrast promises to be a stark one between the present and the past, as it was at the beginning of "The Fire Sermon"; but this is one of several places in the poem where the bringing together of the present and the past does not work merely to the disparagement of modernity. "Elizabeth and Leicester / Beating oars" appear (an impression Eliot's note confirms) a couple engaged in flirty power politics of the most cynical kind, hardly an example of human connection to hold up as a model of good practice.

Between the two verses come some snatches of enigmatic German, which signal Wagner's second substantial appearance in the poem, and suggest a way of understanding the mixed spectacle we have lately witnessed as a perennial state of affairs, such as might be expressed in myth:

Weialala leia
Wallala leialala

The subterranean movements of the poem are absorbing to trace: here, the "gold" of St Magnus Martyr melts into the lucrative business of the river and thence to the "gilded shell / Red and gold" of Elizabeth's sparkly barge, and all in the company of Wagner's Rhinemaidens, who are also creatures of gold. These three water-nymphs first appear in *Das Rheingold*, the opening opera in the *Ring of the Nibelung* cycle, opening the opera with their joyful shrieks of "Wallala weiala weia!" They have been charged with looking after the precious Rhinegold, a task they misconceive as straightforward since no one can take the gold unless he has renounced love, which they take to be inconceivable; but they have not banked on the consuming desire of the evil Alberich, who curses love very readily and is thus empowered to seize the gold, to the maidens' dismay, precipitating the rest of the long story. Eliot's note points us towards the closing opera in the cycle, *Götterdämmerung* ('The Twilight of the Gods'), at the beginning of the third act of which the maidens reappear lamenting their loss and longing for a hero to restore their precious possession: their cry now is, "Weialala leia, / Wallala leialala". Once again, Eliot cuts into the Wagnerian sound-world at the point of deepest loss.

The notes says that the song of the Thames maidens starts at l.266, and that they speak from l.292. They each tell of their undoing – "Richmond and Kew / Undid me" says the first – as their stories track the Thames from Richmond in the West, through the City, and out into the release of the sea by Margate Sands. Eliot's ear for cadence in these verses is perfect, the women speaking with a moving mixture of reticence and worn acceptance:

> *"My feet are at Moorgate, and my heart*
> *Under my feet. After the event*
> *He wept. He promised 'a new start'.*
> *I made no comment. What should I resent?"*

The smallest of grammatical dislocations (properly my heart *is*, not *are*, under my feet) is enough to imply some distraction of mind. The meaningless promise uttered by the weeping lover is beautifully judged in a poem where every new start so far has turned out to be a replication of experience already "foresuffered". Only out towards the open space of the sea may there be some intimation of possible redemption for there, as the third Thames maiden sings: "I can connect /

Nothing with nothing." The lines have that characteristic inscrutability we have now heard several times: is this is a cry of waste land despair – "I am unable to connect anything with anything else" – or does it gesture towards some fuller, joined-up sense that might be made out of "nothing"? A final fragmentary stub of the Thames maidens' lyrical noise ("la la") suggests some exhausted collapse into the near-wordlessness of the lowest point.

At the nadir of his fortunes, as described in his *Confessions*, St Augustine comes to Carthage, where he is beset by "a cauldron of unholy loves", as he says: "To Carthage then I came". Eliot crosses these flames of Christian sin with the burning described by the Buddha in his sermon: "Burning burning burning burning". Later in his *Confessions*, Augustine is able to address God who has saved him from the snares of the body: "but Thou pluckest me out, O Lord, thou pluckest me out". But as Augustine's hopeful words appear in *The Waste Land*, they are puzzlingly contextless and no sooner uttered than repeated in a snapped-off version that renders them meaningless, cut down. There is a powerful sense in these moments of the poem falling into pieces, as though running the normal processes of composition in reverse: "the apparent irrelevance and unrelatedness of things" of which Eliot once spoke taking over any capacity of the mind to gather them into poetic structures. Part III ends with a floating, unpunctuated participle: "burning".

Who is Phlebas? *312-21*

"Death by Water". In one of the most cruelly ironic juxtapositions of the poem, it is as though, with "burning" still burning our ears, the poet were to say: "So you hope for water? I'll give you water." (Eliot would write later, in 'East Coker': "I said to my soul, be still, and wait without hope / For hope would be hope for the wrong thing".) Phlebas, going down the whirlpool, forgets the mercantile life of the water; he is picked apart by currents (picking up on the currants in his Smyrna equivalent's pockets); he suffers the sea-change which Ariel imagines in the song recalled earlier in the poem. The tone of the final injunction is teasing, apparently a sage piece of moral guidance ("Consider Phlebas, who was once handsome and tall as you"); but this feels like a much simpler kind of moral intelligence than the difficulty of the poem has led us to expect. The lines come across as the sort of thing poets used to say.

In the version that Pound received, these three verses came at the end of a long first-person narrative told from beyond the grave about a disastrous sea-voyage ending in a collision with an iceberg. Pound cut all of that, no doubt properly, though one line was sacrificed which deserved to

live: "My God man theres bears on it." This wasn't
the first appearance of the three verses, for an early
version of them had first appeared, in French, as
the ending to another poem by Eliot called 'Dans
le Restaurant': that text made mention particularly
of the tin trade and the swell of Cornish seas –
"la houle de Cornouaille" – and so may have
established a subliminal connection with Isolde
crossing the sea with Tristan. It ended on a
different note, too: "Figurez-vous donc, c'était un
sort pénible; / Cependant, ce fut jadis un bel
homme, de haute taille." ("Imagine it, a terrible
fate; yet he was formerly a handsome man, so
tall.") 'Death by Water' doesn't make much of
his "terrible fate", which adds to the eerily defeated
air of tranquillity about the dissolution of Phlebas.

What is that sound? *322-94*

The opening lines of Part V were the lines with
which Eliot was most pleased: "not only the best
part," he wrote to Bertrand Russell, "but the only
part that justifies the whole at all". Matthiessen
records Eliot speaking in an unpublished lecture
about his ambition

> to write poetry which should be essentially
> poetry, with nothing poetic about it, poetry
> standing naked in its bare bones, or poetry so

transparent that we should not see the poetry, but that which we are meant to see through the poetry, poetry so transparent that in reading it we are intent on what the poem *points at*, and not on the poetry...

And Matthiessen is surely right to suggest that when Eliot went on to refer to "the forty or fifty original lines that I have written" that approach that achievement, it was the opening of "What the Thunder said" that he had in mind.

The first lines seem to be taking place after some catastrophe, "the agony in stony places"; but while the poetry draws on details of Christ's story it remains studiously non-denominational. The poem conveys an unresolved quality at odds with the finality of the things of which they seem to be speaking:

> *He who was living is now dead*
> *We who were living are now dying*
> *With a little patience*

As Ricks says, these lines go through the motions of rhetorical strength in their parallelism, but they arrive at a last line the significance of which refuses to be pinned down, partly because the absence of any punctuation denies us one of the most normal guides to understanding. There is something puzzling, anyway, about the claim to be

dying "with *a* little patience": "with little patience"
would make sense (if one were raging against the
dying of the light) as of course would "with
patience" (were one reconciled to one's destiny);
but "with a little patience" keeps mum about
whether it is the presence of patience at all which
is noteworthy or the limitations of the patience
that there is.

Such suggestiveness comes from the
constraints of a new minimalism: punctuation has
been rationed, and now it seems vocabulary has
been too, as the poetry begins to revolve with
obsessional insistence around a small number of
nouns – rock, water, road, mountains – as though
seeking to exhaust all their possibilities, like a
broken-up sestina, beating, as Empson said of the
sestina, "forever upon the same doors in vain".
This is the arid sub-lyricism of "dry grass singing",
the lines both exhausted and tenacious, struggling
through a lexical desert with inert rhythmical
resources; but they keep going: they manifest a
"poetic art of endurance", in Reeves's phrase.
When water does arrive it does so – a dark joke –
in the form of fluent and lovely singing – the song
of the hermit-thrush, "Drip drop drip drop drop
drop drop". (The garrulous note specifying *Turdus
aonalaschkae pallasii* shares the bleak humour of
the moment: "Its "water-dripping song" is justly
celebrated," says Eliot, as if there were any scope
for *celebration* round here.) But there is no place

for such a voice in this increasingly monotonous, self-bound verbal space, and the song is abruptly terminated with a dour correction of error: "But there is no water".

"Who is the third who walks always beside you?" That meaning should be present but tantalisingly elusive is the point of the eerily atmospheric anecdote that follows, based, as Eliot's notes tells us, on the story of the road to Emmaus as told by Luke, crossed with an hallucination reported from one of Shackleton's expeditions to the Antarctic. In the gospel two disciples travel along in the company of the freshly resurrected Christ, quite clueless as to who he is; and in Shackleton, the exhausted explorers could not resist the delusion that one additional person accompanied them, though never to be directly perceived: both stories imply a tantalising vicinity of significance that cannot be caught or comprehended.

The pressing questions continue as the poem's camera now zooms out and takes in a vast panorama of desolation: "What is that sound high in the air", "What is the city over the mountains" – though by now the interrogative energy of the poem is so diminished it cannot even manage to summon up a question mark. Another of Madame Sosostris's prognostications has come true: here are crowds walking endlessly around within the ring of the horizon. The air, again, is "violet", bringing its earlier implications into play, and associating them now by verbal proximity with the 'violent' forces unleashed in civil turbulence, ancient and modern:

> *Falling towers*
> *Jerusalem Athens Alexandria*
> *Vienna London*
> *Unreal*

That expands the field of the poem to the reiterative dynamics of world history, a change of perspective that seems confirmed by Eliot's note: he refers to *In Sight of Chaos*, by his contemporary Hesse, with its pessimistic portrait of modern Europe collapsing into the abyss, and evidently associating his own interest here with that panicky analysis of current affairs. ("I find in your book *Blick ins Chaos* a seriousness the like of which has not yet occurred in England, and I am keen to spread the reputation of the book," Eliot wrote to Hesse in March 1922.)

So it is probably a bit of a jolt to most readers when the scale abruptly changes again to the more literary and spooky dimensions of "A woman drew her long black hair out tight / And fiddled whisper music on those strings". Eliot's old friend Conrad Aiken remembered reading *The Waste Land* when it first came out and recognising this section (and some others he doesn't specify) as having been

St Magnus Martyr and the monument, Billingsgate, from London Bridge, circa 1900

written long before the main body of the poem, and so "not *organically* a part of the total meaning": just as a matter of genre, you might have guessed it came from a different part of Eliot's mind. But whatever the force of "*organically*" as Aiken uses it, in truth the verse is connected up to the poem at large by many filaments: the air by now is full of self-echoes, the poem "[t]olling reminiscent bells", as Eliot says. The vampiric lady's hair is pulled out "tight" ("Marie, / Marie, hold on tight"); "whisper music" ("[p]icked his bones in whispers"); "the violet light" ("the violet hour"); "beat their wings" ("[a] nother hid his eyes behind his wing"); "towers" ("[w]hite towers"); "bells, that kept the hours" ("St Mary Woolnoth kept the hours"); "empty cisterns" ("no empty bottles".)

The poem is treading in its own footprints, as though coming to a kind of crisis in resources. The "[d]ead mountain mouth of carious teeth" (l.339) is revisited – "that money he gave you / To get yourself some teeth" – and a promising discovery made: in the "decayed hole among the mountains" there is an "empty chapel". Eliot's note relates the chapel, "only the wind's home", to the scene of the Grail quest, but a precise connection to the world of *From Ritual to Romance* seems more distracting than necessary at this stage: what really matters is a growing atmosphere of some vague and imminent event. Gathering up something of the cupola in which the Wagnerian boys sang, and the inexplicable space of St Magnus Martyr, the chapel encloses an emptiness waiting to be filled. A cock crows dramatically, perhaps a little melodramatically; and then, finally, after a long poem that has longed for fresh water, and been given only salt water or sullied water or the water that is wept, we have, if not a proper downpour, then at least "a damp gust / Bringing rain". And then the Thunder speaks.

What does the Thunder say? *395-433*

"Then spoke the Thunder." The Thunder speaks as the voice of God in the Upanishads, the series of philosophical treatises written in Sanskrit that constitute the Hindu scriptures. Eliot had studied Sanskrit for two years at Harvard, ending up, as he later recalled, "in a state of enlightened mystification"; but he hardly anticipated a similar familiarity among his readership. He provides a helpful reference in the endnotes; but, anyway, there is an appropriateness in that the voice of God, among all the troubled European voices that make up the work, should seem the most simply alien and inexplicable; it is something speaking a different language altogether. Eliot, complained Conrad Aiken, wants the words "to be

remembered in connexion with a Upanishad";
but "we have none of us this memory, nor can he
give it to us; and in the upshot he gives us only a
series of agreeable sounds which might as well
have been nonsense". But, as Ricks says, this is
to misunderstand Eliot's design: the thought that
these words might well come across to us as
"nonsense" is anything but "agreeable", and the
calculated discomfort of the experience of reading
these last couple of pages is entirely purposeful.

Eliot rejigged the order of the story from the
Upanishads (the subject is well explored by Cleo
McNelly Kearns); but the gist of the legend is this.
The Thunder roars out its monosyllabic "Da" to
three types of listener, all of whom comprehend it
as the first syllable of a word, but each group thinks
of a different word. Some presume "Datta", which
Eliot says means "give" (as in alms); some
"Dayadhvam", meaning "sympathise" (be
compassionate); and some "Damyata", meaning
"control" (as in self-control): these are the three
ethical imperatives to which, in that order, Eliot
finds his own responses. In the original, the three
groups are men, demons, and gods; but Eliot's
interest remains exclusively human-scaled, and
it picks up on preoccupations that are squarely
his own.

1. *Datta* (give)

The instruction is met at once with a self-reproaching question – "what have we given?" This is much more than a matter of charitable impulse, evidently: the giving at stake is nothing less than a complete act of self-abnegation before the reality of another person, a breaking out from the self-enclosure of personality – just what the tongue-tied man in the hyacinth garden was unable to achieve.

> *The awful daring of a moment's surrender*
> *Which an age of prudence can never retract*
> *By this, and this only, we have existed*

Eliot was a qualified admirer of William Blake, who once averred that "Prudence is a rich ugly old maid courted by Incapacity"; but Eliot's concern is not with the innocence of acting upon desire – he had grave doubts about desire, as we have seen – it was, rather, with the kind of experience he once described in a memorable letter to Stephen Spender:

You don't really criticise any author to whom you have never surrendered yourself... Even just the bewildering minute counts; you have to give yourself up, and then recover yourself, and the third moment is having something to say, before you have wholly forgotten both surrender and recovery. Of course the self recovered is never the same as the self before it was given.

He is discussing literary criticism here, but, as Frank Kermode says, he is describing at the same time something powerfully operative in all aspects of his mind, including his poetic genius – as it is described, for example, in the trailblazing early essay "Tradition and the Individual Talent". The individual poet truly realises his talent at all, says Eliot, only through a process of submission to something greater than himself:

> What happens is a continual surrender of himself as he is at the moment to something which is more valuable. The progress of an artist is a continual self-sacrifice, a continual extinction of personality.

The lines in *The Waste Land* are not primarily absorbed by the problems of art, but rather by the problems of life, and by what properly defines a life – moments of private self-sacrifice which do not feature in the public records of the obituary or last will and testament, presided over by the "lean solicitor".

Of course Eliot is hardly the first to think that you gain your soul by losing your self: "We proceed from the SELF, in order to find and lose all self in GOD," as Coleridge once proclaimed; but God is an extremely elusive presence in *The Waste Land*, and Eliot's tone wins credence by not being simply or merely a vindicatory credo. "By this, and this only, we have existed": yes, that is richly affirmative, a statement of the singular thing ("only") that makes a life worth enduring, but it is a spirituality of very thin pickings – this one moment, this is all that we shall be able to show for ourselves? And Eliot's instinctive anti-sentimentalism means that the price of surrender is never minimised either: "bewildering" is the word he uses to Spender; "awful" is what he says here – full of awe, yes, but also just something you would normally avoid like you would anything awful.

2. *Dayadhvam* (sympathise)

So, the wrong kind of individuality is what you need to evade or to escape in the process of making great art or good literary criticism or making your existence worthwhile. The disconnective world of *The Waste Land* has been both stylistic and moral – "We cannot say at what point 'technique' begins or where it ends" – it is a place where individuality has become a self-confirming imprisonment. Eliot's response to the injunction to "sympathise" draws on a grisly passage in Dante, in which the speaker is locked up in a cell and allowed to starve to death: "and below I heard the door of this

horrible tower being nailed up" (or, as Eliot
seems to have understood the lines, "locked up"):
the self has become a prison, and the lines are
appropriately entrapped within the narrow
compass of their reiterated terms:

> *I have heard the key*
> *Turn in the door once and turn once only*
> *We think of the key, each in his prison*
> *Thinking of the key, each confirms a prison*

Blake, in one of his own poems about London,
spoke of "[t]he mind-forg'd manacles I hear": here,
the mind thinks itself into the incarceration of an
"I". Meaning is locked over the enjambments:
"turn once only" (and won't turn again for the door
to be opened) and then also "only / We think of the
key" (for the key is of our making). Eliot's other
note at this point is to the philosopher Bradley, a
passage describing the individual soul sealed up in
the private sphere of itself: "every sphere is opaque
to the others which surround it".

   That quotation, as Eliot – who had written a
doctoral thesis about Bradley – knew very well,
seriously misrepresents the final position of
Bradley, who wrote with passion about an all-
inclusive and single Absolute into the ultimate
reality of which all partial experiences were
absorbed. The tragic pluralism of experience by
which Eliot is preoccupied in *The Waste Land*

might be better represented by another Victorian writer, Walter Pater, of whom Eliot took a generally low view (which does not preclude him receiving an influence, of course). A famous sentence from the once-controversial "Conclusion" to Pater's book *The Renaissance* overlaps with Eliot's concerns in several respects:

> Experience, already reduced to a swarm of impressions, is ringed round for each one of us by that thick wall of personality through which no real voice has ever pierced on its way to us, or from us to that which we can only conjecture to be without. Every one of those impressions is the impression of the individual in his isolation, each mind keeping as a solitary prisoner its own dream of a world.

Pater accepts this chilling picture with an odd breezy acceptance: in a way, his exquisite aestheticism is a matter of making the best of it; and that is where Eliot does not choose to follow him. If there were to be any ghost of a hope, it was not going to lie in the fetishising of solitary experience.

Eliot's rhymes work to enclose: "key"/"only"; and then one of the best of all the Eliotic dead-rhymes, "prison"/"prison"; but then at the end, a sudden break into new acoustic space:

Only at nightfall, aethereal rumours
Revive for a moment a broken Coriolanus

Again, any consolatory sentiments on offer are very hard-won in these lines, a matter of rumours: again, the sparse condition of an "only" at once elevates the "moment" into something uniquely precious while also confirming its lamentable uncommonness.

Coriolanus is the last Shakespearean character we will meet, an unlikely crescendo perhaps as he is one of the most difficult of the tragic heroes. A dreadful Roman military superstar, Coriolanus is the fierce conqueror of the Volsces, Rome's bitter enemies, with whom, in a startling *volta-face* motivated by pride and contempt, he then joins forces and returns, threatening to sack his own city. He faces an unforgiving choice between two acts of betrayal: he can attack Rome, ignoring the passionate entreaties of his mother, or he can relent, in which case his fate is sealed at the hands of his thuggish new allies.

None of this feels very close to the interests of *The Waste Land*, but what Eliot must have had in mind was the extraordinary pivotal moment in the play in which, following an immense barrage of rhetoric from his ferocious mother, Coriolanus finally chooses not to sack Rome after all. It is his greatest moment, his defining moment, and simultaneously entails his certain destruction; but the real dramatic power of the episode lies less in the quandary and more in the fact that, in the midst of a play heaving with the remorseless articulacy of Roman power-politics, Coriolanus appears to take his decision in a pause of quite wordless connection. As his mother comes to the end of her last tirade, the stage direction, the most descriptive in the Shakespeare First Folio, reads: "*He holds her by the hand, silent*". And then the world of rhetoric wheels back into place once again: "O mother, mother! / What have you done?" The whole play pivots on Coriolanus's silence, at once self-destructive and self-redemptive, which seems to have communicated with the silences in Eliot's poem, places where language runs out, through lassitude ("Why do you never speak") or indifference ("I made no comment") or incapacity ("I could not / Speak").

3. *Damyata* (control)

Perhaps mindful of Shakespearean hands, the marine fragment which responds to 'control', draws together the "hand" that sails a boat with the "hands" of a lover. The language of the "heart" here ventures upon the erotic: now it is not one's own heart that matters – "and my heart / Under my feet", "blood shaking my heart" – nor the heart as a numinous abstraction ("the heart of light"), but someone else's heart. The lines are as close as the poem dare come to the romantic idiom of, say, Browning's "two hearts beating each to each". In the spirit of the responsiveness they imagine, the lines attend to one another: "responded / Gaily" is returned as "would have responded / Gaily"; but the regretful conditional confesses an act undone.

The poem then comes to a catastrophe of fragments, as though pushing the method of the poem to a crisis at its close. The tentativeness that has marked all three responses to the Sanskrit is now enforced by a larger tentativeness about what progress might have been represented by their utterance: it seems that no rain has arrived after all. The "limp leaves / Waited for rain" before the Thunder started; and now we find a fishing figure (a re-appearance of the fisherman of l.189?) with a still "arid plain" behind him. That the fisherman takes some inspiration from Jessie Weston does not seem so very helpful: no key is going to "set... in order" the cacophony of competing voices that we encounter now. (Eliot would later say of the "music of poetry" that "dissonance, even cacophony, has its place".)

These fragments are all garbled recollections of what has gone before, a delirious version of the poem in miniature. The "[f]alling towers" and the commuters on London Bridge are scrambled in the scrap from the nursery rhyme; and the towers will return again in "[t]he Prince of Aquitaine, of the tower in ruins", a snippet from the French poet

Nerval. Meantime, a line from Dante's *Purgatorio*, describing a penitent throwing himself willingly back into the fire to make good his lustful sins, revisits the penitent fiery experience of St Augustine. Apparently randomly, "[w]hen shall I become like the swallow?" asks an anonymous medieval voice in Latin; and "O swallow swallow", chimes in the speaker in Tennyson's love story, *The Princess*; but both actually show that Philomela is always on his mind: as Philomela is changed into a nightingale, her sister Procne, who commits the revenge, is magicked into a swallow. "These fragments I have shored against my ruins": is that to say that something has been propped up and made secure again, or just that the best had been made of a crumbling job? "Why then Ile fit you. Hieronymo's mad againe": it is from *The Spanish Tragedy* by the Elizabethan playwright Kyd. Hieronymo has been driven mad by the murder of his son and has written a play, in which the killers are cast; and the play has a peculiar characteristic which no doubt stuck somewhere in Eliot's mind:

> Each of us must act his part
> In unknown languages,
> That it may breed the more variety.

A striking covert movement of the imagination brings the poem to its close while returning to the terms of its opening: "breeding / Lilacs out of the dead land".

"These fragments I have shored against my ruins": the unusual construction ("shore up" would look more normal) insinuates a grammatical wobble and alerts us, as by a pun, to the awareness that this peace ending the poem is anything but sure. The Sanskrit is repeated, as though ceremonially; and then we have the closing phrase of an Upanishad, to which, as Eliot's note glosses, the Christian expression "The Peace which passeth understanding" is the equivalent – or, as he said in the first version of the notes, "a feeble translation of the content of this word". The word certainly has an immense significance within Hindu tradition, one which it is difficult for Western readers to grasp; but then that is a tradition from which this poem is frankly excluded, and the tantalising sense of a spiritual plenitude being withheld is a key part of the effect.

The implication of the phrase and its true intonation here are as difficult to establish as they are for many of the most haunting utterances in this elusively voiced work. Might there be something missing? According to Kearns the end to an Upanishad is properly "Om shantih shantih shantih", which would mean that Eliot's ending secretly contains within it a gesture admitting incompleteness. Eliot's note tells us the phrase is "a formal ending to an Upanishad", which cuts the matter nicely: is this the way to end with all due formality, or is it merely a matter of form? "The very end, and yet not," Ricks says, "since after as many as five full-stops within the antepenultimate and penultimate lines, perfect peace asks no punctuation. Here is no formal ending."

Is *The Waste Land* a pessimistic poem?

So then, what are we to feel as we arrive at the end of this hesitantly ended poem? One question to ask might be: is it a pessimistic poem? Its view of contemporary Europe is bleak, and reflects Eliot's strong personal sense of deepening historical catastrophe: "Having only contempt for every existing political party, and profound hatred for democracy, I feel the blackest gloom," he wrote to a friend in April 1921; and when the young Stephen Spender asked him, a few years later, what future he foresaw for civilisation, Eliot replied: "Internecine fighting... People killing one another in the streets."

But the poem has a double focus, a little like 'Dover Beach', Matthew Arnold's great Victorian poem of isolation, which describes both a contemporary malaise and a perennial state of affairs – what Arnold calls "the eternal note of sadness"; and Eliot's sense of the devastation inherent in human lives, too, far exceeds a painfully keen awareness of the historical travails of his time. After he had become a member of the Church in 1927 the imagery of the waste land continued to appear in his poetry: in Eliot's sparsely consolatory form of Christianity, religion does not irrigate the waste away but rather places it within a universe in which its unhappiness finally makes a kind of sense.

> The desert is not remote in southern tropics,
> The desert is not only around the corner,
> The desert is squeezed in the tube-train next to
> > you,
> The desert is in the heart of your brother.
> > ('Choruses from the Rock' [1934], I)

You could not say that Christian hope irradiated Eliot's post-conversion poetry: "Men and bits of paper, whirled by the cold wind / That bellows before and after time" ('Burnt Norton') are visited ever only fleetingly by moments of redemptive possibility – "Not known, because not looked for / But heard, half-heard, in the stillness / Between two waves of the sea" ('Little Gidding').

And yet something not unlike a half-heard voice of redemptive experience was to be heard in *The Waste Land* too. "The awful daring of a moment's surrender / Which an age of prudence can never retract / By this, and this only, we have existed": saying so might appear to suggest that what makes a life worth enduring is a colossal, rare, act of the spirit, a "moment" of decision so transformative that it enables you to wring a meaning from existence, the creation of your own audacious will. That sounds a bit like the radical individualism of Nietzsche – as when, in *The Gay Science*, Nietzsche imagines a demon arriving at your loneliest moment to tell you that you are foredoomed to lead your life over and over again, in every minute detail – in "every detail of desire, temptation, and surrender", as Eliot's original epigraph from Conrad put it. How do you answer? Do you curse the demon for so unimaginably dreadful a fate? Or, alternatively, says Nietzsche,

> have you once experienced a tremendous moment when you would have answered him: "You are a god and never have I heard anything more divine"?

That is magnificent; but it is important to grasp how completely different it is, really, from Eliot, for whom the "moment" that transforms existence is not a climax of individual self-justification but a momentary abandonment of the self altogether. The mistrust of individualism that we have seen in *The Waste Land* is one of the foundations of Eliot's mind. To attempt to depend upon the resources of the individual self – what he sometimes called, without admiration, "the inner voice" – is to lean upon nothing but personal errancy and self-delusion: the "Inner Light", as he says at one point, is "the most untrustworthy and deceitful guide that ever offered itself to wandering humanity".

His Christianity, accordingly, when it comes, is profoundly anti-individualistic: there is very little sense of a transforming relationship with the person of Christ, say, nor of the redeeming agency of the crucifixion; and certainly nothing remotely like the strange warming around the heart that marked the arrival of Christ in the breast of John Wesley. There is, instead, as Eliot puts it in 'The Dry Salvages',

> hints and guesses,
> Hints followed by guesses; and the rest
> Is prayer, observance, discipline, thought and
> action.

The Waste Land had portrayed a wilderness of individualities; but it glimpsed the transformative power of a 'surrender' to something greater. In the essays Eliot was writing around the period of the poem, that greater thing was sometimes called 'tradition' or "the mind of Europe... a mind which he [the poet] learns in time to be much more important than his own private mind" ("Tradition and the Individual Talent"); and 'tradition' remains a presence in later writings, where the self may also be set to find its significance within the greater something of orthodoxy, or the Church, or a rooted culture. But in *The Waste Land*, in the absence of those candidates, the domain of possible hope remains precariously within the human.

The poem is certainly mindful of Wagner's extraordinary insistence that erotic love itself has the power to transfigure existence and to redeem even death; and though it is unable to rise to such heights itself, *The Waste Land* has nowhere to look other than personal relationships for something in which for the time being to place all its needy, unfulfilled hopes. "The experience of a poem is the experience both of a moment and of a lifetime," Eliot would later write in his great essay on Dante, his thoughts then returning, for the moment, to his masterpiece, "blood shaking my heart / The awful daring of a moment's surrender". ("*Ego dominus tuus*" – I am your master – is what Love says to Dante in the *Vita Nuova*.)

It is very much like our intenser experiences of other human beings. There is a first, or an early moment which is unique, of shock and surprise, even of terror (*Ego dominus tuus*); a moment which can never be forgotten, but which is never repeated integrally; and yet which would become destitute of significance if it did not survive in a larger whole of experience; which survives inside a deeper and a calmer feeling.

CHRONOLOGY

1888 26 September, Born in St Louis, Missouri.

1906 Enters Harvard University.

1910 Graduates from Harvard; travels to Paris and attends lectures at the Sorbonne. Meets Jean Verdenal.

1911 Visits London. Returns to Harvard to do a PhD in philosophy. Writes 'The Love Song of J. Alfred Prufrock', 'Portrait of a Lady', and 'Preludes'.

1914 Arrives at Merton College, Oxford, on a visiting fellowship. Meets Ezra Pound.

1915 Marries Vivien Haigh-Wood. 'Prufrock' published in *Poetry*, through the offices of Pound. Settles in England.

1916 Teaches at Highgate School.

1917 Joins Lloyds Bank. *Prufrock and Other Observations* published.

1919 *Poems* published by Leonard and Virginia Woolf at the Hogarth Press.

1920 *The Sacred Wood*, a collection of critical essays, published.

1921 During the autumn, Eliot's health breaks down and he is given three months' leave. He travels to Margate in October, and to Lausanne in November, during which time he drafts *The Waste Land*.

1922 Visits Paris at the beginning of the year where Pound

revises the manuscript. Eliot resumes work at the bank. He completes the final version, which is published in Britain in the first number of *The Criterion*, a literary and cultural journal edited by Eliot, in October, and in the USA in *The Dial*. It appears as a book in America in December.

1923 *The Waste Land* is published as a book by the Hogarth Press in England.

1925 Leaves Lloyd's Bank to work at the publishers Faber and Gwyer (soon to be Faber and Faber).

1927 Joins the Church of England and becomes a British citizen.

1930 'Ash-Wednesday' published.

1935 His play, *Murder in the Cathedral*, first performed.

1936 Publishes 'Burnt Norton'.

1938 Vivien Eliot, who has been certified insane, is committed to a lunatic asylum.

1939 *Old Possum's Book of Practical Cats* published.

1943 *Four Quartets* published as a volume.

1947 Vivien Eliot dies.

1948 Awarded Nobel Prize in Literature.

1957 Marries Valerie Eliot.

1965 4 January, dies.

FURTHER READING

Editions

Collected Poems 1909-1962 (1963).

The Waste Land: A Facsimile and Transcript of the Original Drafts including the Annotations of Ezra Pound, ed. Valerie Eliot (1971).

The Waste Land: Authoritative Text, Contexts, Criticism, ed. Michael North (2001).

The Waste Land and Other Poems, ed. Frank Kermode (2003).

The Annotated Waste Land with Eliot's Contemporary Prose, ed. Lawrence Rainey (2005; second edition, 2006).

Commentary

B.C. Southam, *A Student's Guide to the Selected Poems of T.S. Eliot* (1968; sixth edition, 1994).

Other Works by Eliot

The Sacred Wood: Essays on Poetry and Criticism (1920).

Collected Poems, 1909-1962 (1963).

Selected Prose of T. S. Eliot, ed. Frank Kermode (1975).

Inventions of the March Hare: Poems 1909-1917, ed. Christopher Ricks (1996).

The Letters of T.S. Eliot, ed. Valerie Eliot, Hugh Haughton, John Haffenden (2009- present. Volume I contains Eliot's letters up to 1922).

Some Criticism and Scholarship

Cleanth Brooks, '*The Waste Land*: An Analysis'; in B. Rajan (ed.), *T.S. Eliot: A Study of his Writings by Several Hands* (1947).

Ronald Bush, *T.S. Eliot: A Study in Character and Style* (1983).

Denis Donoghue, *Words Alone: The Poet T.S. Eliot* (2000).

William Empson, *Seven Types of Ambiguity* (1930).

— 'My God Man, There's Bears on It'; *Essays in Criticism* 22 (1972), 417-29; collected in *Using Biography* (1984).

Barbara Everett, 'Eliot's Marianne: *The Waste Land* and its Poetry of Europe'; *Review of English Studies* NS 31 (1980), 41 -53.

Helen Gardner, *The Art of T.S. Eliot* (1949; 1968).

Lyndall Gordon, *Eliot's Early Years* (1977).

Michael Grant (ed.), *T.S. Eliot: The Critical Heritage*, 2 vols. (1982).

Cleo McNelly Kearns, *T.S. Eliot and Indic Traditions: A Study in Poetry and Belief* (1987).

Hugh Kenner, *The Invisible Poet : T.S. Eliot* (1960; 1974).

F. R. Leavis, *New Bearings in English Poetry: A Study of the Contemporary Situation* (1932; 1950).

F. O. Matthiessen, *The Achievement of T.S. Eliot: An Essay on the Nature of Poetry* (1935).

Craig Raine, *T.S. Eliot* (2006).

Lawrence Rainey, *Revisiting The Waste Land* (2005).

Gareth Reeves, *T.S. Eliot: A Virgilian Poet* (1989).

— *T. S. Eliot's The Waste Land* (1994).

Christopher Ricks, *T.S. Eliot and Prejudice* (1988).

Allen Tate (ed.), *T.S. Eliot: The Man and his Work* (1967).

INDEX

I am grateful to the many authors who have written so well about Eliot's poem, especially Gareth Reeves and Christopher Ricks; and I thank Jason Harding for his kind help. I owe an immense debt to Jacqueline Baker, to whom this book is dedicated.

First published in 2014 by
Connell Guides
8th Floor, Friars Bridge Court
Blackfriars Road
London SE1 8NZ
10 9 8 7 6 5 4 3 2 1

Picture credits:

A CIP catalogue record for this book is available from the British Library.
ISBN 978-1-907776-27-4

Design © Nathan Burton
Assistant Editors:
Katie Sanderson & Pierre Smith Khanna
Printed in Great Britain by Butler, Tanner and Dennis

www.connellguides.com